MW00379897

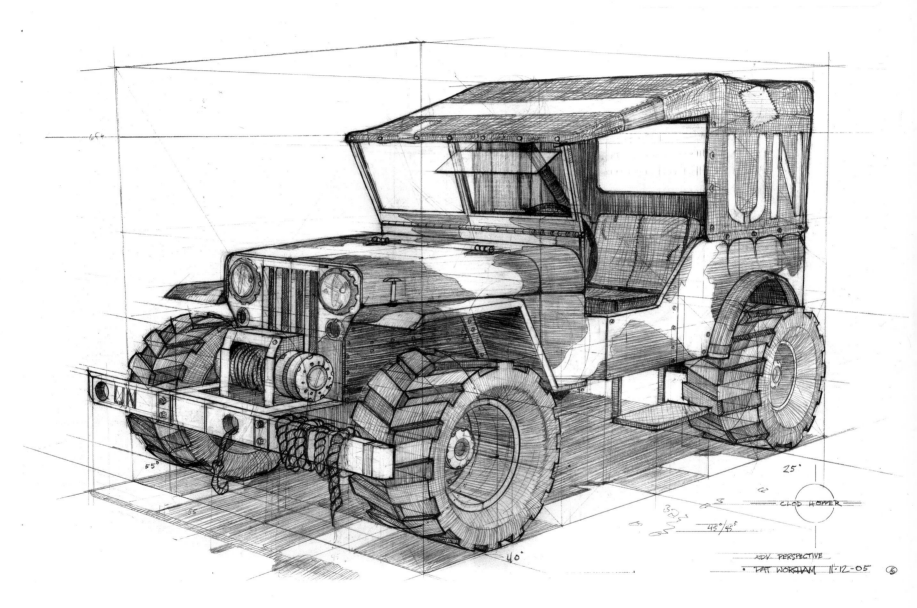

6ft

UN

UN

55°

40°

25°

CLOD HOPPER

45/45

ADV PERSPECTIVE
PAT WORSHAM 11-12-05

in the future...

ENTERTAINMENT DESIGN
AT ART CENTER COLLEGE OF DESIGN

BY SCOTT ROBERTSON & THE INAUGURAL CLASS
OF ENTERTAINMENT DESIGN AT ART CENTER COLLEGE OF DESIGN

designstudio PRESS

dedication

This book is dedicated to aspiring concept artists everywhere.

Jeep sketch on first page by Pat Worsham
Title page image by Peter Chan

Copyright © 2006 by Design Studio Press

All rights reserved.
No part of this book may be reproduced or transmitted in any form or by any means, electronic or mechanical, including photocopying, xerography, and videography recording without written permission from the publisher, Design Studio Press.

All illustrations in this book are copyright © 2006 by J. Bach, D. Bacon, P. Chan, M. Collins, D. Hobbins, H. Kasom, S. Katayama, S. Ko, F. Lacey, E. Lutes, E. Ng, J. Pichetrungsi, R. Rihal, S. Shatz, C. Shoji, K. Swartz, T. Tenery, L. Truong, G. Whitehall, P. Worsham V. Ying.

Art Direction: Scott Robertson
Graphic Design: fancygraphics
Web Site: www.fancygraphics.net

Layout Production: Marsha Stevenson
Text Editor: Kevin Brown

Published by Design Studio Press
8577 Higuera Street
Culver City, CA 90232

Web Site: www.designstudiopress.com
E-mail: Info@designstudiopress.com

10 9 8 7 6 5 4 3 2 1

Printed in China
First Edition, December 2006

Paperback ISBN-13: 978-1-933492-17-9
Paperback ISBN-10: 1-933492-17-1
Hardcover ISBN-13: 978-1-933492-18-6
Hardcover ISBN-10: 1-933492-18-X

Library of Congress Control Number:
2006922590

contents

foreword

I have always been captivated by the future unknown: by the vast potential that it holds and the fact that we are limited in its realization only by the constraints of our imagination. Visual development is the responsibility to bridge the gap between what we know and where the future lies, expanding the realm of the possible by making it visually accessible.

With these heady responsibilities, emerging designers need to have an ever-expanding arsenal of abilities and skills, both technical and creative, with which to solve these visual puzzles and create a coherent visual direction. There is no question that there are many technical advancements which have given modern designers the tools to create more, quicker and slicker; but what is most important is the ability to manipulate these tools to express new visual directions and not simply replicate what has already been done. Good draftsmanship and illustration skills are requirements for this. The final key ingredient, which cannot be taught, is the desire to constantly push the credible and the unfettered vision to see it.

It is a great solace to me to know that veterans of my generation will be passing the responsibility to see—and in seeing, create— the future to emerging designers of the caliber showcased in this volume. With the skills represented here by these students I have no doubt the future of visual development is in good hands.

Steven Olds

Creative Director, Rock Star Games

Fall 2006 / New York

Over the past 75 years, Art Center College of Design has been a leader in the educating of tomorrow's entertainment designers. Located in the Los Angeles area, it has been at the heart of one of the most creative environments for art and design in the world. With a long history of guiding young illustrators and industrial designers with an eye for "the movies," Art Center has been contributing to the field of entertainment design for quite some time: a long list of graduates such as Syd Mead, Nick Pugh, Harald Belker, Ryan Church, Neville Page, Mark Goerner, James Clyne, Sean Hargreaves, and Farzad Varahramyan, to name just a few, have all gone on to pursue legendary careers in the field.

Until recently, students interested in working in the entertainment design field would pursue their studies at Art Center by mixing equal doses of illustration and industrial design classes, with the intent of building a portfolio to get them concept design work in feature animation, video games or live-action film productions. This has now changed. At the request of Nathan Young, Executive Vice President and Chief Academic Officer, I put together an entertainment design curriculum that would bridge the gap between industrial design and illustration, providing students with an interest in this field a clear path to achieving their goals. In the fall of 2005, we launched our first class of students into this new program at Art Center. With students from both the industrial design and illustration departments in the same classes, I believe that the program is working well to fuse the two disciplines; providing more focused and specific education geared to preparing top-notch conceptual designers for the entertainment industry.

Historically speaking, industrial designers' skills tend to be weakest in several areas important to being a successful concept designer for the entertainment industry—figurative work, picture composition, color theory, and narrative illustration. Conversely, the illustration students have been historically weak in technical perspective drawing, object styling, model building and design methodologies. Our new entertainment design program aims squarely at improving these weaknesses of each discipline.

Skilled concept designers for the entertainment industry are tasked with designing and illustrating characters, environments, vehicles and props that the world has never seen before. In addition, they are required to provide the documents necessary for these objects, characters and worlds to be built by other team members. This requires a strong understanding of how things are built and having the ability to communicate this through drawings; this is the part of the job that relies more on their industrial design skills. To show narrative aspects of the designs, the designers' illustration skills are required to rise to the occasion. Simply put, the concept designers of tomorrow will be expected to have the ability to design and skillfully illustrate unique and compelling characters, environments, vehicles and props for stories taking place in past, present, and future time periods. No small task to accomplish with only five terms dedicated specifically to this goal.

In the following pages you can read a more detailed description of the Art Center entertainment design courses being offered over those five terms. What you will find in the rest of this book is a presentation of just some of the work that has been done by the fourth- and fifth-term students who are taking part in the new program. Please keep in mind as you look at the work, and read the commentary provided by the instructors at the beginning of each chapter and by the student's themselves throughout the chapters, that this book represents a work-in-progress preview of the types of exciting topics being pursued by the students. Personally, I think the work is worthy of showcasing and I am enthusiastic about the next book from this group of students—the one that will feature their finished work after another three terms of study in the program at Art Center College of Design.

I hope you enjoy our presentation of some of the student work in this very exciting new discipline as much as I have been enjoying both the great energy and positive attitude of these fine students.

Scott Robertson.

Scott Robertson

Entertainment Design Program Director

Fall 2006 / Los Angeles

Entertainment Design at Art Center College of Design

1ST THROUGH 3RD TERMS

During the first three terms at Art Center, students will be focused on the completion and mastering of the design, drawing and rendering foundation program. Upon a successful completion of this program the students will submit a portfolio for review in order to gain admittance into the Entertainment Design program. Upon acceptance into the program they will proceed through the following outline of courses below. For more detailed and up-to-date course information visit: **www.artcenter.edu/datalog** and query the Programs of Study.

4TH TERM

Color Theory
Course material covers the properties and effects of light and color during different times of day and under various lighting conditions, as well as complex color properties such as luminosity, iridescence and transparent overlay.

Imaginatomy
Even though most character development is done on computer, it is imperative for students to explore the 3-dimensional "common sense" of organic forms in a hands-on way. This class will explore anatomy and zoological similarities and differences in a variety of animals. By studying their mechanics, students will observe how levers and fulcrums function.

Advanced Perspective
In this course the technical aspects of how to draw various objects and environments through the traditional practice of freehand perspective drawing techniques will be explained.

Originality in Design
This course will focus on some of the techniques used to create a unique form language that can then be applied to the design of environments, characters, vehicles and props for the entertainment industry.

5TH TERM

Visual Development
This course focuses on quick sketching, editing, and pitching ideas geared towards entertainment design. The primary goal of this class is to provide students with a clearly directed methodology to facilitate the generation of non-derivative work and to familiarize students with the creative process as it specifically applies to the entertainment industry.

Character Design 1
In this course students will be introduced to what characteristics make up iconic good and evil characters. The course will focus on the design on human characters for stories both existing and imagined by the students.

Architectural Design 1
In this course many exterior architectural styles will be presented to the students. In the presentation of each style, design elements of each will be discussed via reference images. After the design elements of any one genre have been communicated to the students they will be expected to communicate through drawings of an architectural exterior of their own design expressing the specific styling guidelines for that genre.

Visual Communication 5 for Entertainment Design
This course will deal with the stylization and rendering of the figure in context of the practice of entertainment design. Students will complete a number of assignments from imagination and observation.

Vehicle and Prop Design	In this course students will be taught the basics of industrial design strategies and techniques for the creation of vehicles and props for the entertainment industry. Past, present, and future time periods will be investigated through a range of design exercises.
Character Design 2	In this course students will be introduced to what characteristics make up believable creatures. The course will focus on the design of creatures for stories both existing and imagined by the students. A strong understanding of anatomy and purpose to each creature will be of particular focus.
Architectural Design 2	In this course many interior architectural styles will be presented to the students. In the presentation of each style, design elements of each will be discussed via reference images. After the design elements of any one genre have been communicated to the students, they will be expected to communicate, through drawings of an architectural interior of their own design, the specific styling guidelines for that genre.
Visual Communication 6 for Entertainment Design	In this course advanced digital rendering techniques will be introduced to the students in both the Painter and Photoshop programs. Shortcuts to increase rendering productivity will be discussed and demonstrated. The techniques of introducing the use of other mediums such as photography and primitive 3-D models will also be widely used.

7TH TERM

Advanced Entertainment Design Studio	In this course students will work on the visual development of characters, environments, vehicles and props for a specific story. The focus of the final presentations in this class will be on the concise and detailed communication of all aspects their designs as related to the building of the those designs in 3-D.
Digital Landscape Painting	During this course students will be painting digitally on lap top computers from observation at variety of locales around southern California. The class will focus on introducing and improving the skills and strategies employed to create compelling imagery from life.
Visual Storytelling	The concept of "visual storytelling" dates back to the origins of mankind. From the first cave paintings to the visual depiction of historic events in temples and churches, ancient societies have chosen the visual medium to communicate their stories to their fellow man. Today more than ever, visual communication dominates our everyday lives.
Costume Design	In this course students will be introduced to the design strategies and techniques employed when designing costumes for a wide range of characters. The course will focus on the design of costumes for human characters for stories both existing and imagined by the students. Design exercises will not only cover a wide range of costumes specific to the purpose of the character they are for but for time periods, past, present and future.

8TH TERM

Entertainment Design Senior Project	In this course students will be presenting the topic of their self-determined area of design study for their last term. After an accepted design brief has been approved, the students will proceed to complete as much of the work as they can achieve by the end of the term. Design objectives and schedule milestones will be agreed upon early in the term on a case-by-case basis with the instructor.
Visual Communication 8 for Entertainment Design	In this course students will be primarily supporting the design work being done for their senior projects. In addition, an emphasis on speed, accuracy and achieving a professional level of visual communication skills will be practiced. All mediums will be supported and explored as appropriate for the specific projects.

Scott Robertson:

Featured in this chapter are selected works from the classes Character Design 1 and 2. In these two classes we cover a very broad range of characters. Character Design 1, with instructors Hong Ly and Kevin Chen, addresses humanoid characters and Character Design 2, taught by Neville Page, focuses on creatures.

In building a student portfolio, it is important to have some projects that involve familiar stories so that everyone reviewing the work will be able to immediately identify and evaluate the designs in context to the story. You will see this throughout the chapter with some of the examples coming from a redesign of the characters for *The Wizard of Oz*. The intention of the classes is to cover all three main types of character design for entertainment: animation, video games and live-action films.

You will see that a strong sense of anatomical study is placed on the development of the creatures within Neville's class. Even though the students were asked to develop original creatures of their own design, it is our belief that without a strong anatomical foundation for the basis of these designs, they will lack true believability.

In the coming terms the students will continue to expand and refine their character design abilities as they progress into costume design class and visual story-telling class. It is the goal of the program to provide assignments that require all of the students to delve into many areas of character design.

Neville Page:

I would like to think that I push myself creatively, but so often I am humbled by the vision of a student. This class, in particular, was a real treat. It is truly one of the greatest aspects of teaching; having the opportunity to see through the eyes of a student. My goal was to give them a deeper understanding of the characters that they would design, both from the physical/anatomical side, and, just as importantly, the psychological/emotive side. Empowered with that, and only then, can the designer begin to create. And, although I would prod and direct, each student was the captain of their own creative ship. Whether they know it or not, liked it or not, they too were teaching me.

INDIAN TIGER OX by Jonathan Bach

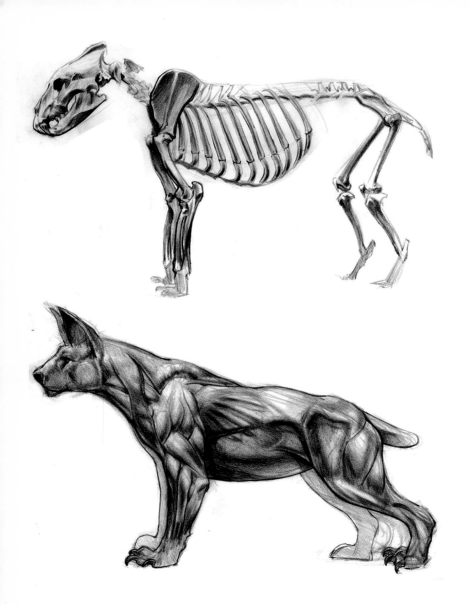

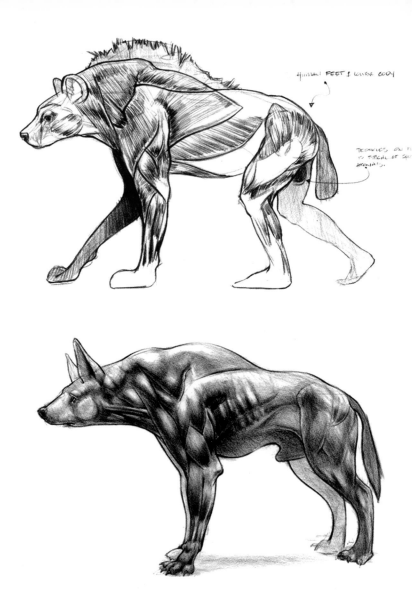

HUMAN FEET & KNEE BODY

TECHNIQUES ON T...
IS TYPICAL OF SO...
ANIMALS...

ANATOMICAL QUADRUPED STUDIES

Shae: Working from the inside out is a great way to gain more understanding of the subject matter you are drawing. On this page, I was creating creatures based on existing anatomy in real animals. The animal above is based on a lion's anatomy, and the skeletal structure on the top was the first stage of design. The three animals on the right side are at various stages of developing a hybrid hyena/dog anatomy. Once I have a solid drawing, I take the design to the final stage as demonstrated in the digital rendering on the right.

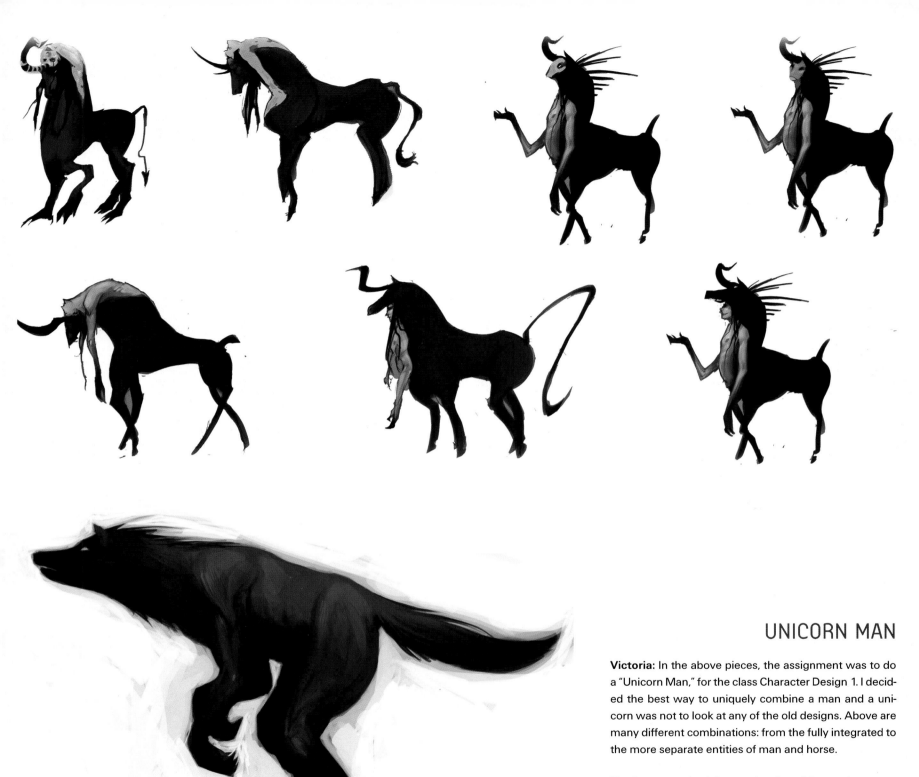

UNICORN MAN

Victoria: In the above pieces, the assignment was to do a "Unicorn Man," for the class Character Design 1. I decided the best way to uniquely combine a man and a unicorn was not to look at any of the old designs. Above are many different combinations: from the fully integrated to the more separate entities of man and horse.

The image to the left was developed in a unique way. First I roughly sculpted the character in order to visualize what it would look like in 3-D. Then I took a photo of the sculpture and painted on top of the photo.

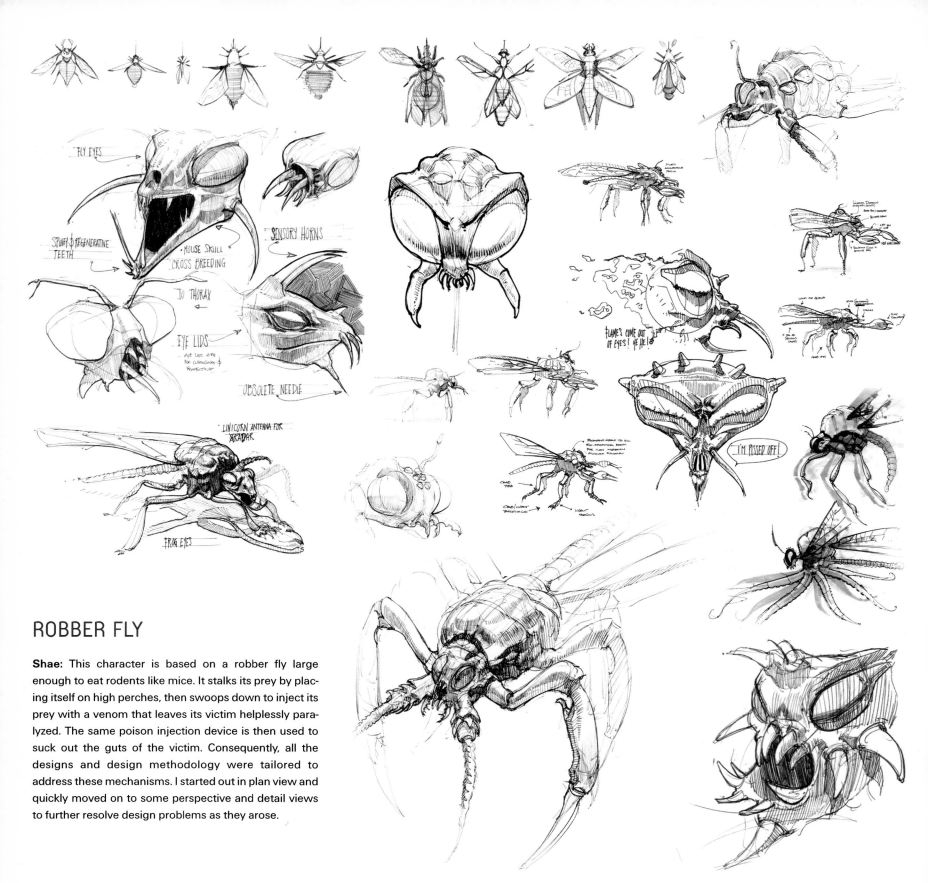

ROBBER FLY

Shae: This character is based on a robber fly large enough to eat rodents like mice. It stalks its prey by placing itself on high perches, then swoops down to inject its prey with a venom that leaves its victim helplessly paralyzed. The same poison injection device is then used to suck out the guts of the victim. Consequently, all the designs and design methodology were tailored to address these mechanisms. I started out in plan view and quickly moved on to some perspective and detail views to further resolve design problems as they arose.

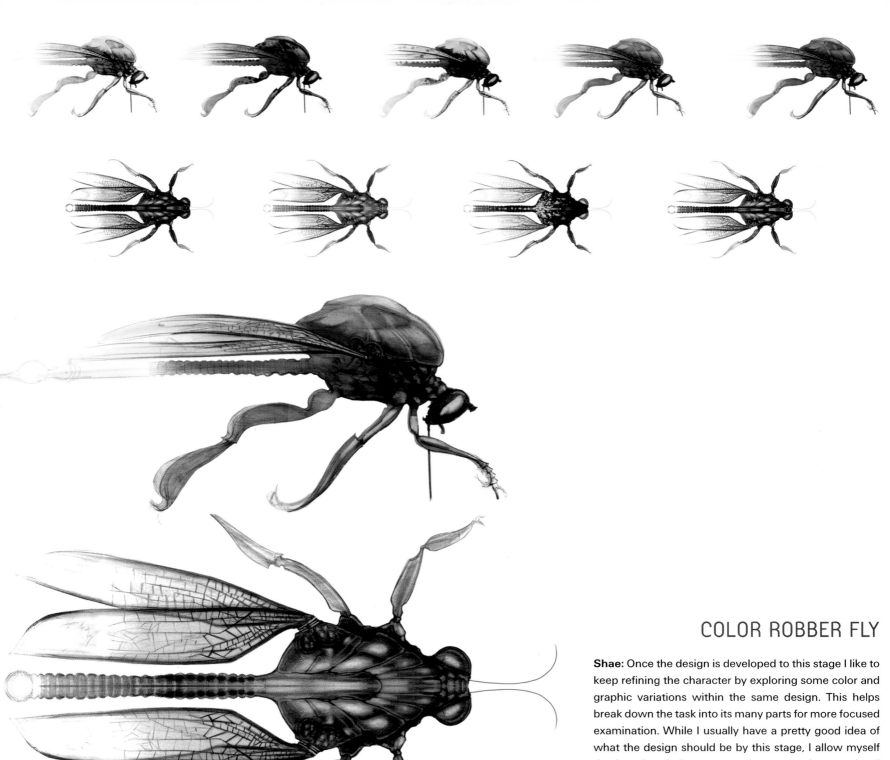

COLOR ROBBER FLY

Shae: Once the design is developed to this stage I like to keep refining the character by exploring some color and graphic variations within the same design. This helps break down the task into its many parts for more focused examination. While I usually have a pretty good idea of what the design should be by this stage, I allow myself the fun of exploring many options, even the occasional silly ones!

SHAE SHATZ

WERETIGER

Lidat: Being a Weretiger, this character was supposed to be humanoid. These are early ideation sketches exploring subtle differences and variations for posture, general stance, and muscle structure. Most of the variations are in the shoulder positioning and posture, which help control the character's feel. Is he heroic, proud, fast and agile, or a bit of a bruiser? Clearly our perception depends upon the variation.

THE SENTINEL | WICKED WITCH

Raj: The boar above is one of the foot soldiers our hero encounters and battles in his journey to rescue the daughter of Zeus, Athena. The design is meant to convey a simple graphic statement that is recognizable both quickly and from a distance. I wanted to express a great deal of danger and power with this character. In addition, I wanted there to be no confusion as to which "end" of our beast was the one to watch out for!

The design to the left is an exploratory sketch for the Wicked Witch from *The Wizard of Oz*. In the process of exploring her "wickedness" I allowed my line work to take on a frenetic and haphazard quality. I wanted her overall shape not only to be jagged, but uncontrolled, expressing her anger, villainy and power.

Wheel Man /Betrayer

Loose Canon

Leader /Skill Position

Intel

Techi

HEISTS | JEKYLL & HYDE

Sho: For Jekyll & Hyde, on the facing page, I designed the figures based on the concept that Jekyll is a prison for Hyde. Jekyll is extremely rigid and his clothes are tight while Hyde has a dangerous stare and weakened limbs like a released prisoner.

The images on this page were developed for "Heists project," for which I developed my own story about a museum robbery. I designed these characters after the process of making the robbery plan, illustrating each role, and writing the backstory to substantiate motivation. The process helped the characters have tangible personalities. I would like to say thanks to the instructor, Ryan Meinerding, for what I learned through these projects.

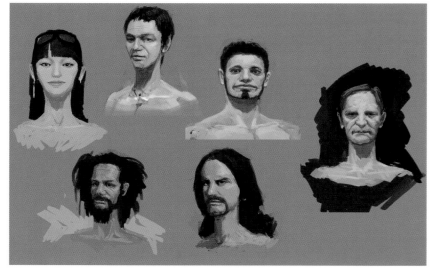

SHO KATAYAMA

SHO KATAYAMA

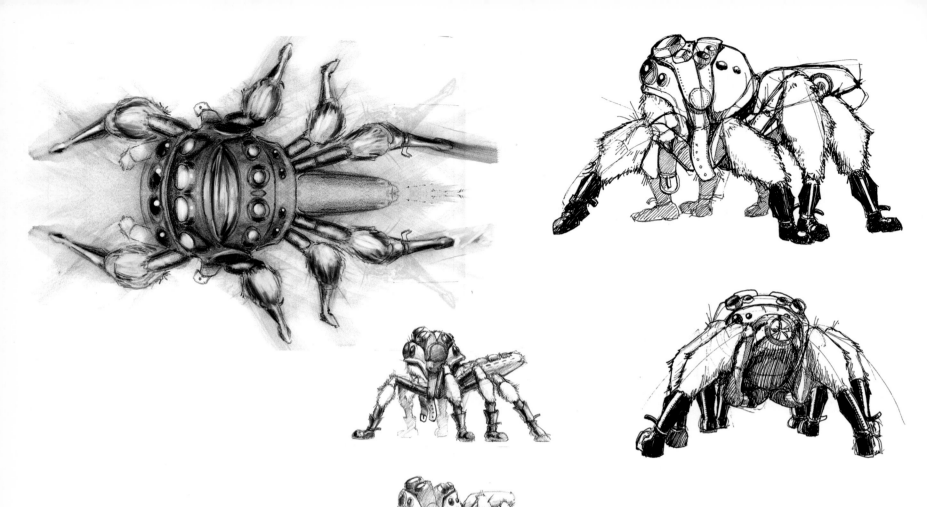

BRITISH WWII JUMPING SPIDER

Simon: I am fascinated by spiders. They have unique textures and hair when you observe them up close. Some can dive underwater and some can leap incredible distances. Some are the size of dinner plates while others can fit onto the head of a pin. This variety made designing with them fun because many things were possible that could still be valid in nature.

After a few hours of sketching, I drew what resembled a spider wearing a leather helmet, not unlike those a Russian WWII pilot would wear. The furry fangs, pedipalps and the pair of appendages near the mouth of a spider resemble a mustache, so I exaggerated them. Almost instantly, I began to speak in a British accent and my RAF WWII jumping spider had come to life.

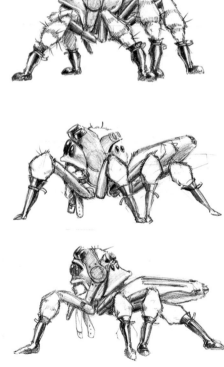

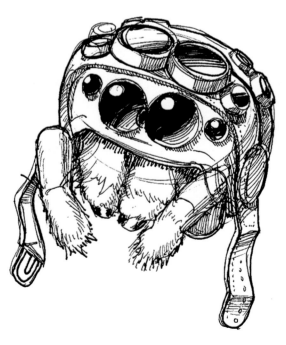

SIMON KO

CHUPACABRA

Simon: Most people are familiar with the Chupacabra, a creature of Mexican cultural myth that sucks the blood of livestock. Here, instead of sucking blood, mine sucks eyeballs. And instead of attacking livestock, it preys on small children who don't go to bed when they are told.

This Chupacabra is a nocturnal arboreal predator that leaps onto its victim, wraps its prehensile tail around the victim's neck, and proceeds to suck the eyeballs out with its long snout and forked tongue. Its long neck is used to bob its head side to side prior to attacking, while judging distance with its excellent binocular vision, much like a cheetah does.

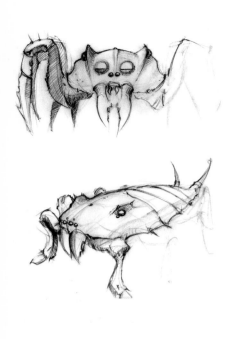

MINING SPIDER

David: For Character 2 class, Neville Page had us focus on the creation of an original insect species. After looking around at various inspirational reference materials, an image of an Orb Spider caught my eye. I thought it would be interesting to modify this spider's unusual abdominal section into a drill. My Mining Spider drills tunnels into soil, then waits for other insects to enter where they would be caught on a sticky cord. The spines radiating from the abdominal section can be articulated to remove soil during drilling or to cage prey. Neville was insistent that the biomechanics of the drill-like section be plausible, presenting a fun and interesting challenge. I explored many loose ideation sketches before committing to orthographic views. The final rendering was completed in Photoshop; textures were created using flower patterns.

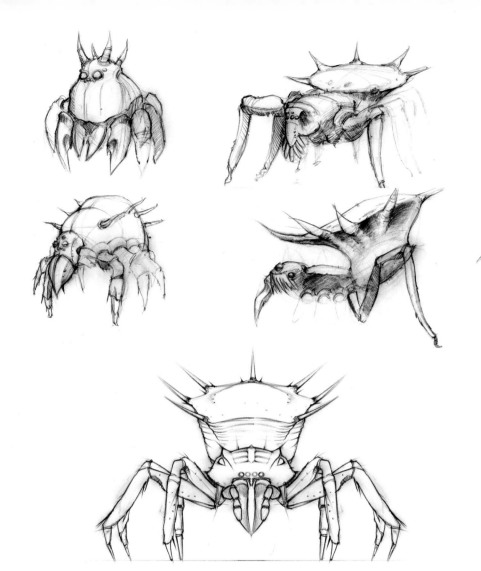

DAVID HOBBINS

DAVID HOBBINS

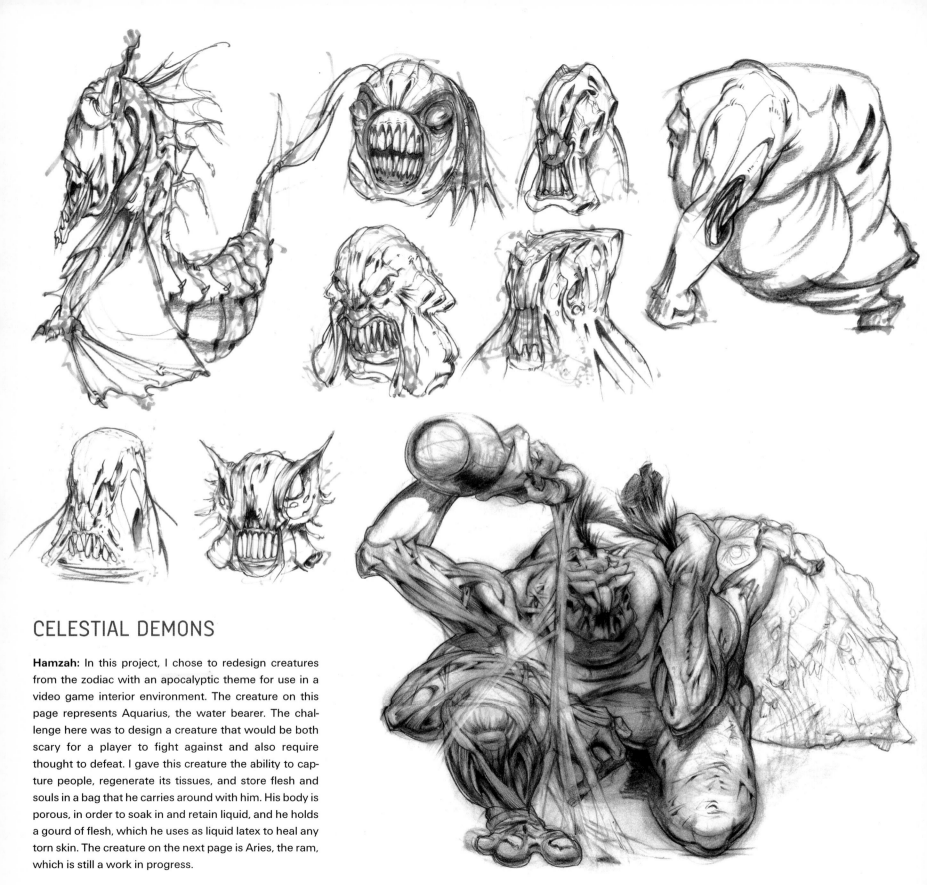

CELESTIAL DEMONS

Hamzah: In this project, I chose to redesign creatures from the zodiac with an apocalyptic theme for use in a video game interior environment. The creature on this page represents Aquarius, the water bearer. The challenge here was to design a creature that would be both scary for a player to fight against and also require thought to defeat. I gave this creature the ability to capture people, regenerate its tissues, and store flesh and souls in a bag that he carries around with him. His body is porous, in order to soak in and retain liquid, and he holds a gourd of flesh, which he uses as liquid latex to heal any torn skin. The creature on the next page is Aries, the ram, which is still a work in progress.

HAMZAH KASOM

HAMZAH KASOM

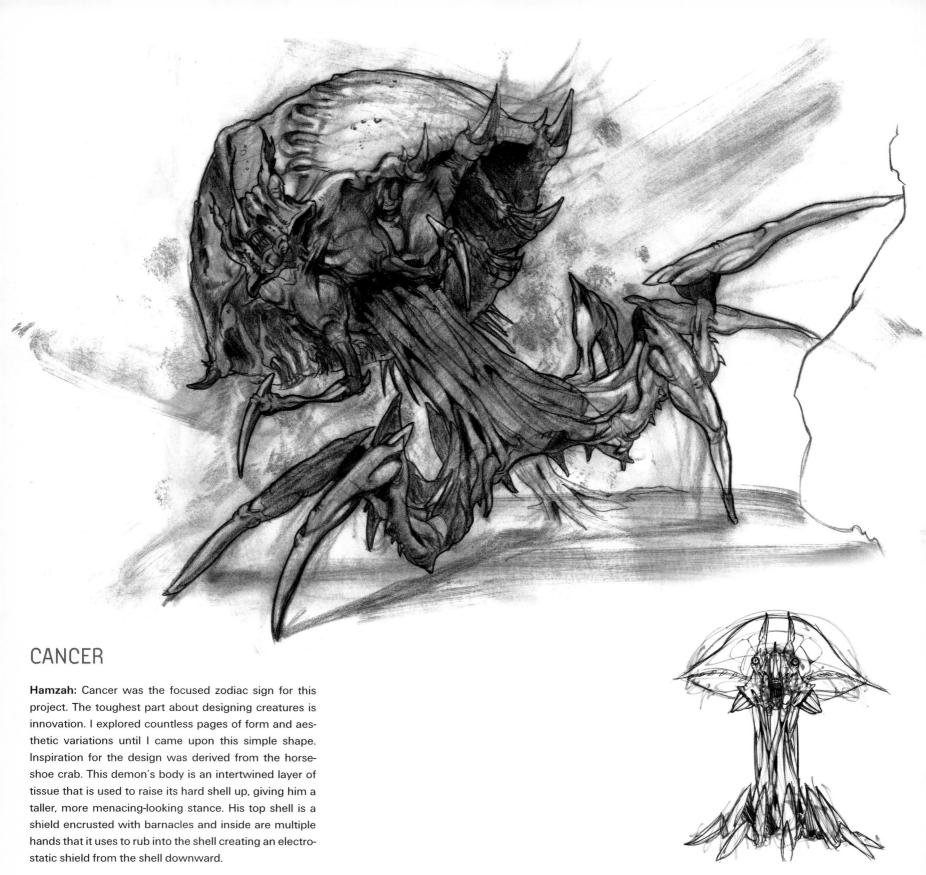

CANCER

Hamzah: Cancer was the focused zodiac sign for this project. The toughest part about designing creatures is innovation. I explored countless pages of form and aesthetic variations until I came upon this simple shape. Inspiration for the design was derived from the horseshoe crab. This demon's body is an intertwined layer of tissue that is used to raise its hard shell up, giving him a taller, more menacing-looking stance. His top shell is a shield encrusted with barnacles and inside are multiple hands that it uses to rub into the shell creating an electrostatic shield from the shell downward.

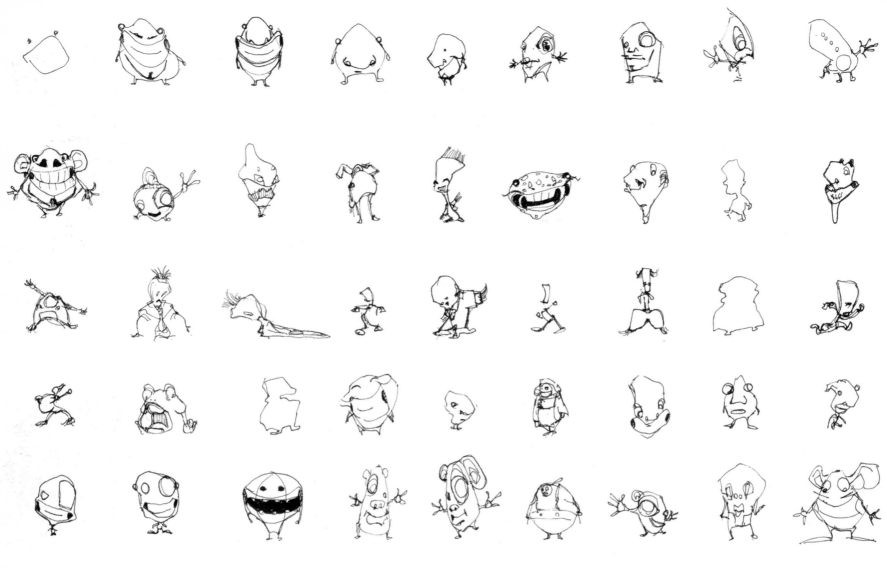

MUNCHKINS 01

Fabian: When redesigning *The Wizard of Oz* characters, I started with the preliminary sketches on the right. These initial thumbnails were no bigger than one centimeter tall. Keeping the sketches that small was the only way I could rapidly teach myself how to simplify my designs. This process allowed me to later define the visual style I would use for the rest of the project. By placing over 200 tiny sketches per page in my sketchbook, I could quickly evaluate and eliminate the weaker designs and further develop the personalities for the stronger ones.

FABIAN LACEY

MUNCHKINS 02

Fabian: On this page are some of the personalities that were developed from the preliminary sketches on the facing page.

Squeeeeeee! Vbububb ubb – noisy little critters they are. There is no way to tell how many of these guys will surround you once in Oz. Thankfully these friendly folks will cause you no harm; they are just curious to meet new-found visitors.

I love when I can get a smile from somebody looking at my work. On this page, the Munchkins are smiling back.

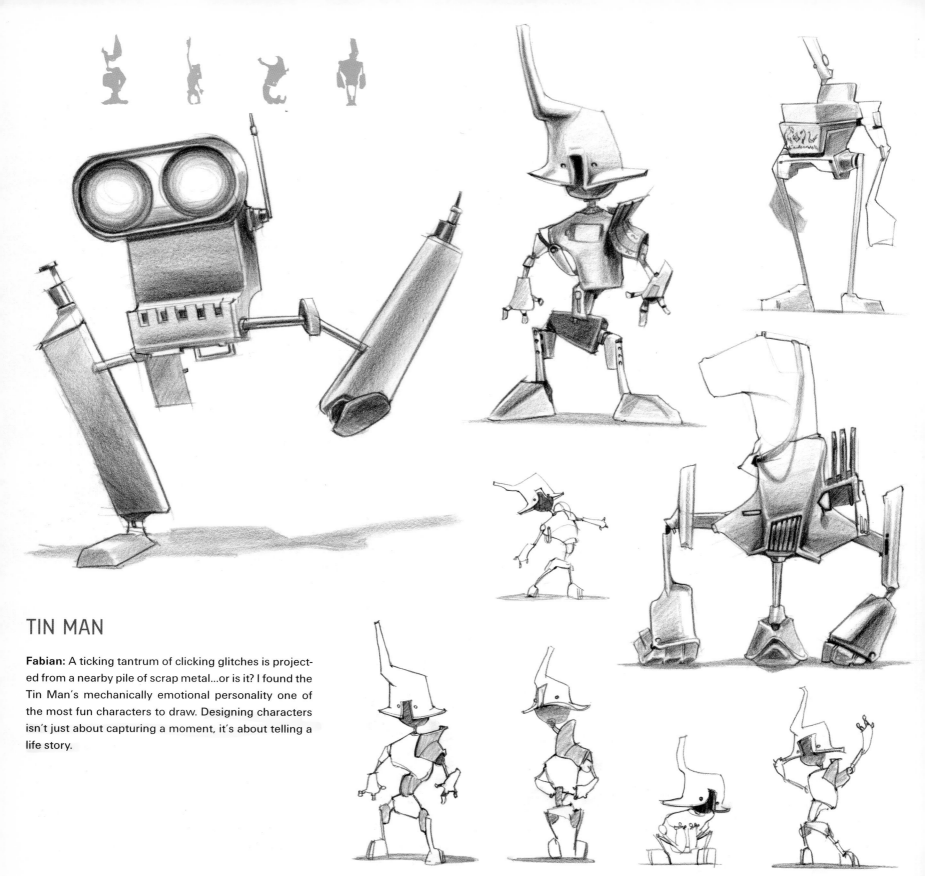

TIN MAN

Fabian: A ticking tantrum of clicking glitches is projected from a nearby pile of scrap metal...or is it? I found the Tin Man's mechanically emotional personality one of the most fun characters to draw. Designing characters isn't just about capturing a moment, it's about telling a life story.

FABIAN LACEY

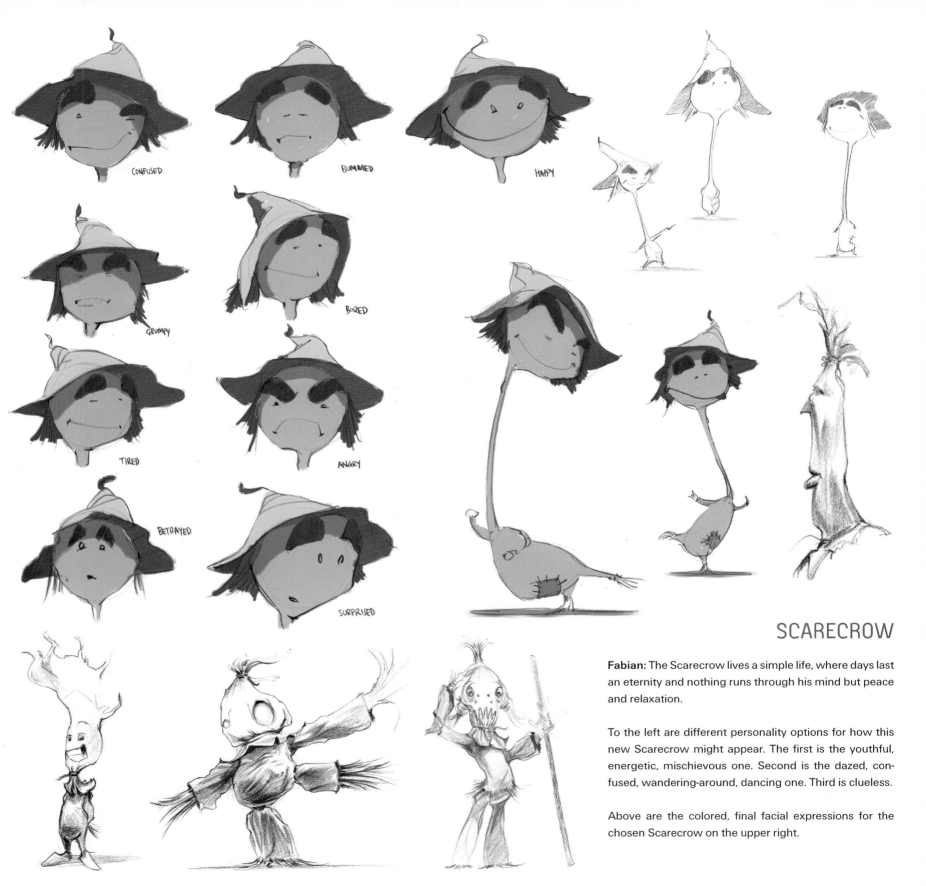

CONFUSED

BUMMED

HAPPY

GRUMPY

BORED

TIRED

ANGRY

BETRAYED

SURPRISED

SCARECROW

Fabian: The Scarecrow lives a simple life, where days last an eternity and nothing runs through his mind but peace and relaxation.

To the left are different personality options for how this new Scarecrow might appear. The first is the youthful, energetic, mischievous one. Second is the dazed, confused, wandering-around, dancing one. Third is clueless.

Above are the colored, final facial expressions for the chosen Scarecrow on the upper right.

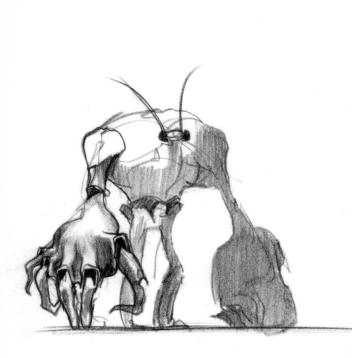

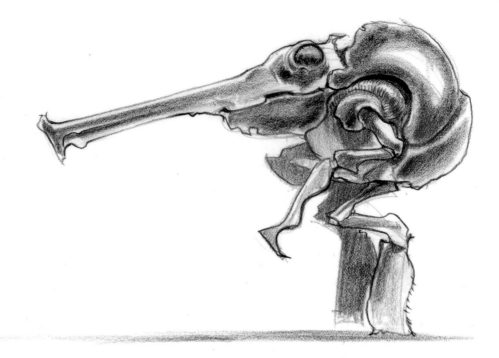

INSECTS

Fabian: Insects are one of nature's ugliest beauties. They come in every size, shape, and form imaginable. They are the jewels of Mother Earth's creations and can be some of the most decorative and ornamental exhibits that roam the planet.

For a video-game development project, Character Design 2 called for an insect. In this exercise, my goal was to ensure that each insect had an exaggerated physical feature that would become its weapon during gameplay.

FABIAN LACEY

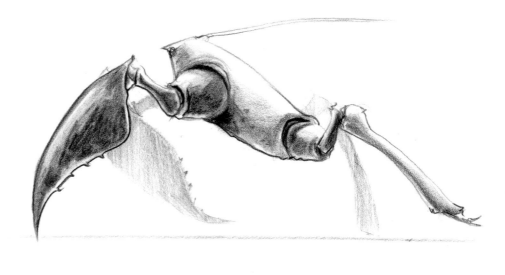
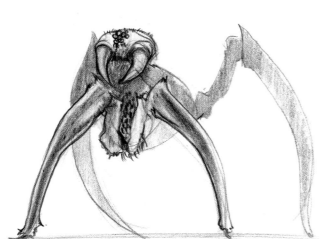
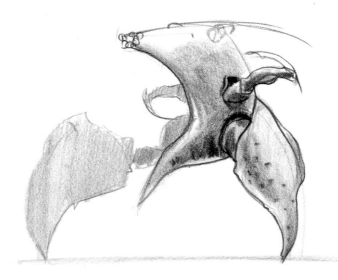

INSECTS

Fabian: Once the weapons for the insect character had been established, I needed to address how it would move. After looking through many references on beetles and crabs, I did the sketches on this page. The design considerations I made were slightly different variations of the legs for moving about on land. Depending on the terrain, each of the characters would have its own strengths and weaknesses.

FABIAN LACEY

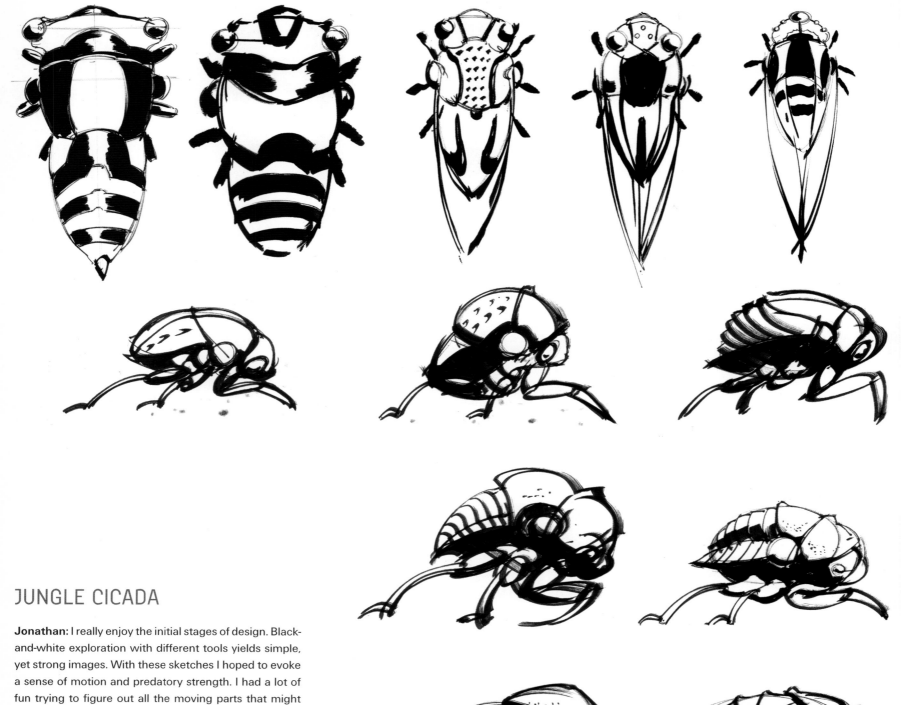

JUNGLE CICADA

Jonathan: I really enjoy the initial stages of design. Black-and-white exploration with different tools yields simple, yet strong images. With these sketches I hoped to evoke a sense of motion and predatory strength. I had a lot of fun trying to figure out all the moving parts that might make up my cicada's mouth. I ended up going with trap doors hiding a pair of small limbs for stabbing and holding prey, along with another rasp-like pair for greedily shoving food into its mouth.

JONATHAN BACH

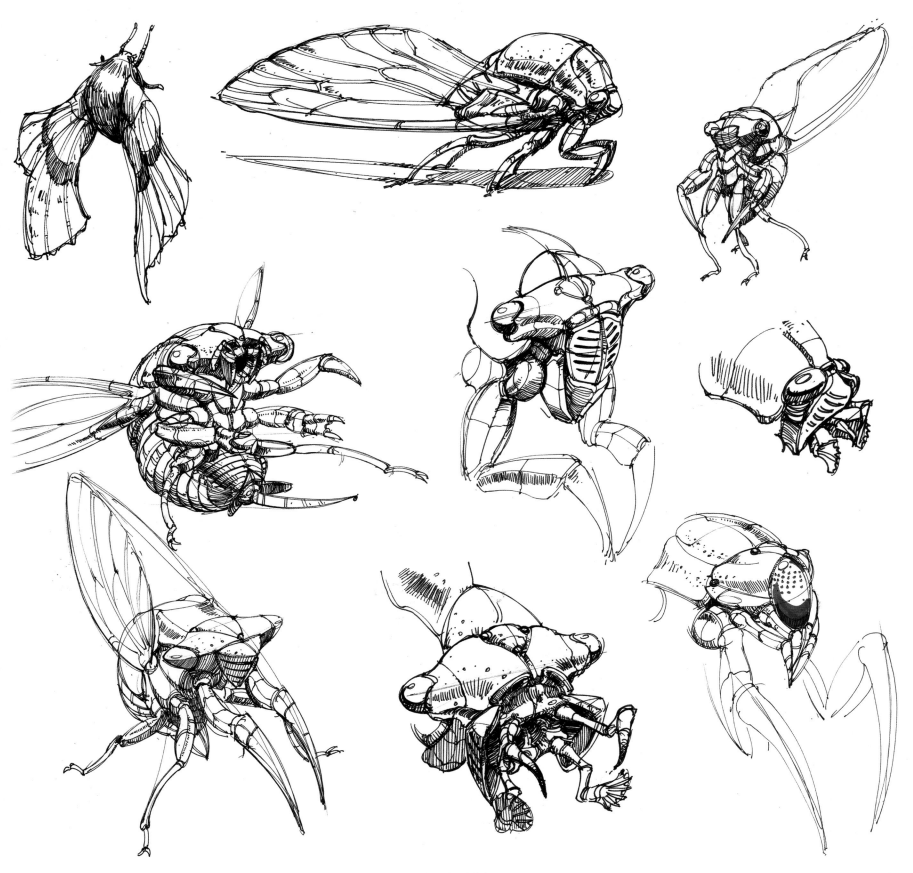

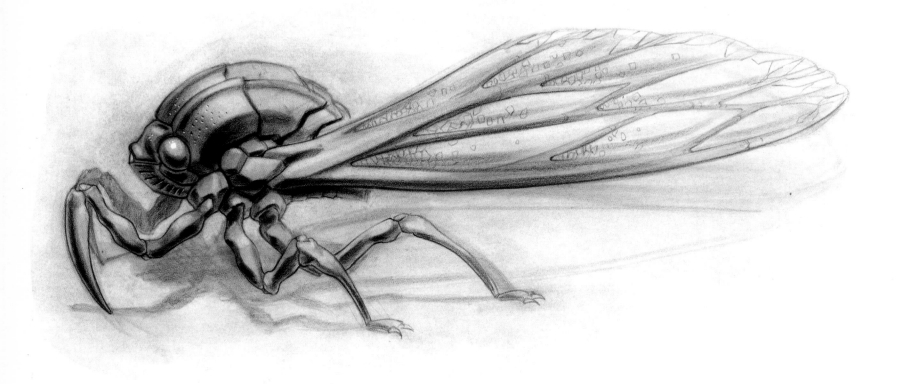

JUNGLE CICADA

Jonathan: One thing that was challenging about creating a new insect was trying to come up with new solutions for its surfaces. I wanted its shell to be new and interesting; however it took me awhile to do that and still make it look natural. In the attempt above I gave the surfaces a faceted look. While it was visually interesting it was still quite unnatural. After a swift kick in the pants from the instructor Neville Page, I hit the reference books and was able to come up with surfaces that worked with the form and looked natural.

JONATHAN BACH

JUNGLE CICADA

Jonathan: The image of the jungle cicada feeding on a boar's carcass uses simple principles of light and color to focus the eye on its subject. The whole of the image is grouped in a darker value range than the mid-tones and highlights of the insect; these areas also have a concentration of color saturation. In addition to that, the subject is in clear focus while the surrounding elements of less interest fall into blurriness. If the foliage in the background had been left in focus the details would have been distracting. By putting the foreground and background out of focus, the image is able to clearly communicate with depth and realism.

SULFORA

Jonathan: With most manufactured items, as with everything in nature, form follows function. Creating a creature from another world can be no different. To start the design process, I used questions like what kind of intelligence does it have? How does it get from one place to another? What kind of food does it eat and how is it metabolized? Is it even carbon-based? These questions helped me form the fuzzy image I had of this creature in my head into something more tangible. The image on the facing page was the culminating answer to the numerous questions that I asked myself during the creative process.

JONATHAN BACH

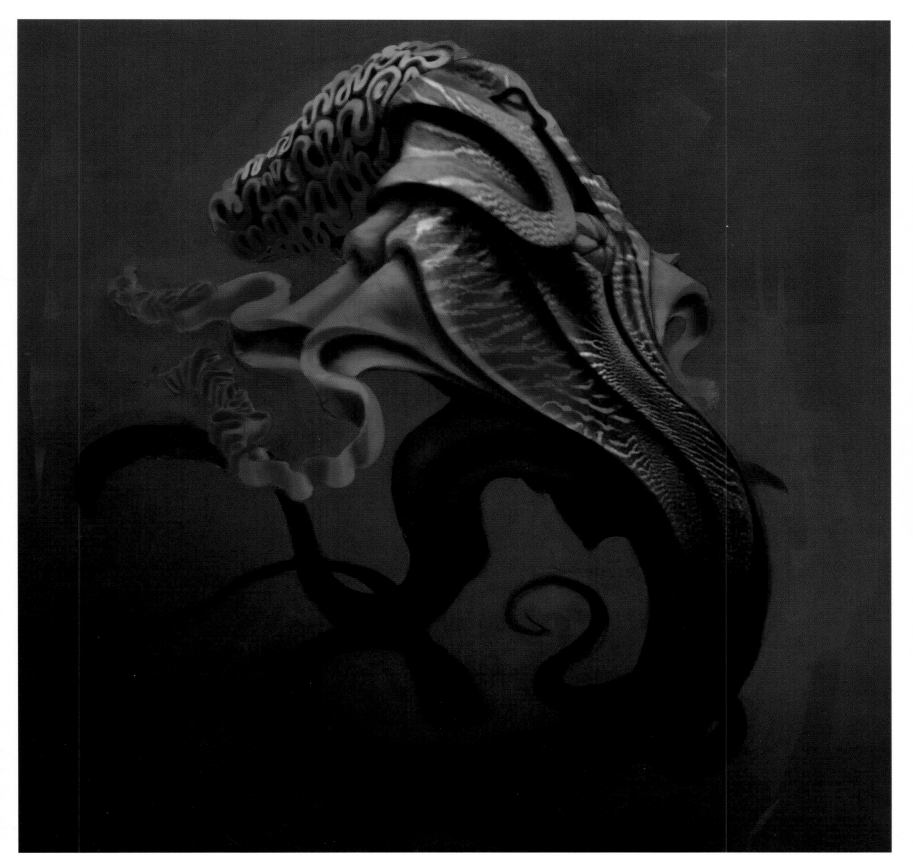

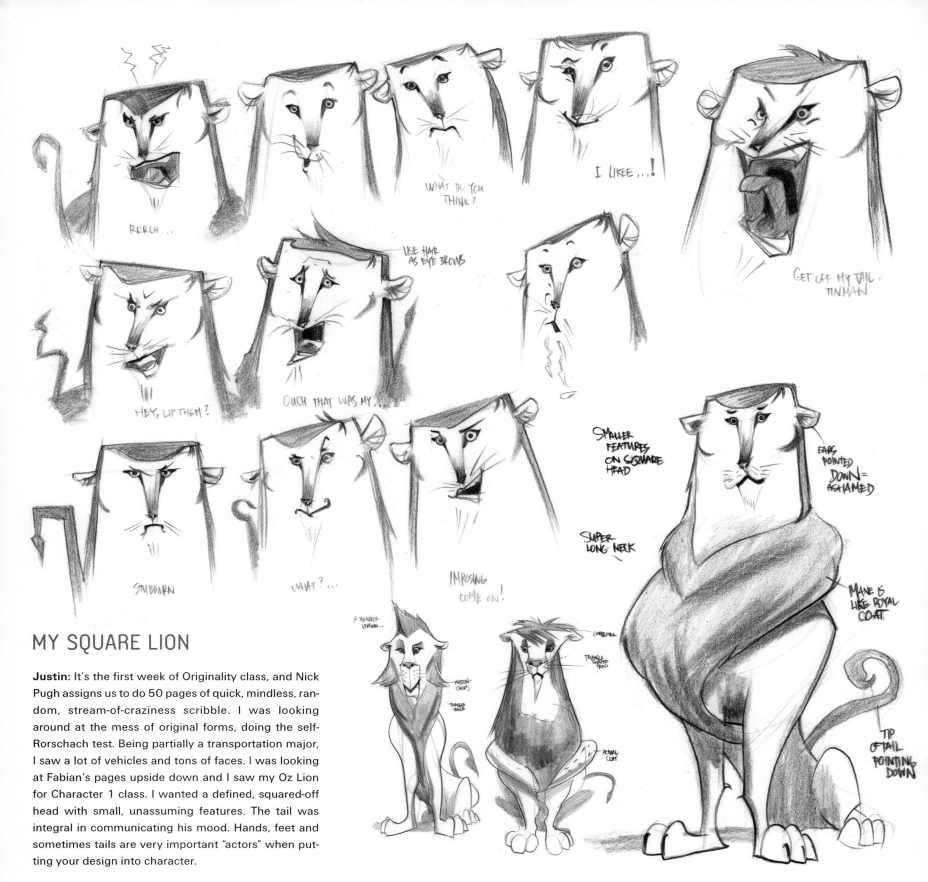

RRRLH...

WHAT DO YOU THINK?

I LIKEE...!

GET OFF MY TAIL TINMAN

USE HAIR AS EYE BROWS

HEY, LIP THEM?

OUCH THAT WAS MY...

STUBBORN

WHAT?...

IMPOSING COME ON!

SMALLER FEATURES ON SQUARE HEAD

SUPER LONG NECK

EARS POINTED DOWN = ASHAMED

MANE IS LIKE ROYAL COAT

TIP OF TAIL POINTING DOWN

A THINNER VERSION...

MUTTON-CHOPS

TRIANGLE SMILE

COMB OVER

TRIANGLE SHAPED HEAD

ACTUAL COAT

MY SQUARE LION

Justin: It's the first week of Originality class, and Nick Pugh assigns us to do 50 pages of quick, mindless, random, stream-of-craziness scribble. I was looking around at the mess of original forms, doing the self-Rorschach test. Being partially a transportation major, I saw a lot of vehicles and tons of faces. I was looking at Fabian's pages upside down and I saw my Oz Lion for Character 1 class. I wanted a defined, squared-off head with small, unassuming features. The tail was integral in communicating his mood. Hands, feet and sometimes tails are very important "actors" when putting your design into character.

DUAL PROPELLER
VTOL MONKEY

DISPROPORTIONATE
WINGS.

MOHAWK

THE CANES

A SLIGHTLY
CONFUSED
+ MENTAL
MONKEY

PIERCING

THE ROCKER
MONKEY
MIGHT HAVE A BANANA
GUN BASED ON A
GUITAR

CAST DESIGN

Justin: Above is a preliminary, silhouetted cast line-up. One of the major critiques that Kevin Chen and Hong Ly gave me is that characters never stand alone. It is key to design characters that live and breathe within a cast. These protagonists' shapes will be interacting with the antagonists' shapes. The cast is the whole design, and each character is merely a cog in the design. Just as a single character design plays up the straights vs. curves, and contrasting and harmonizing forms, so must the cast design. Even elements like the values and colors of the characters should not be fully contrasted within each character, but within the whole of the cast.

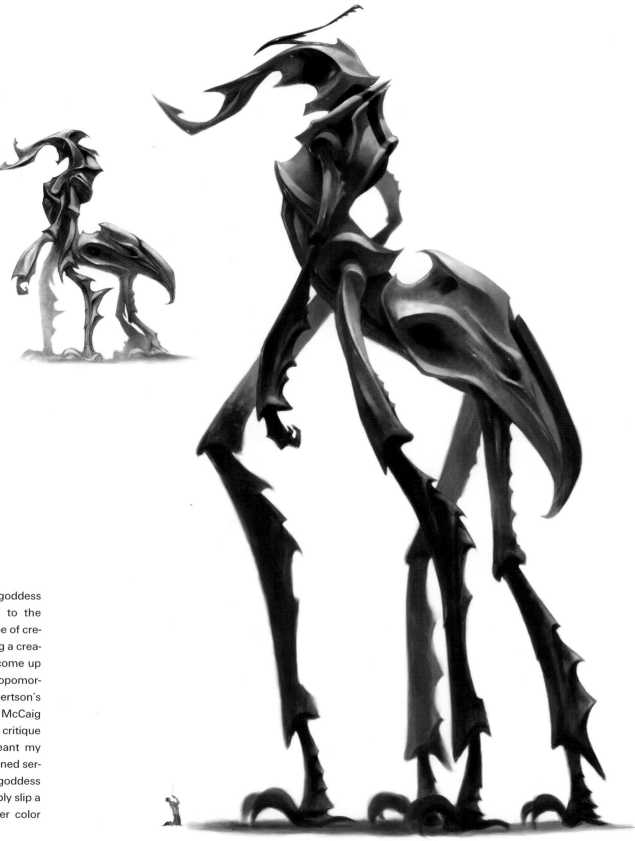

VITRUSA

Justin: This is a concept for a stag beetle goddess named Vitrusa, whose totalitarian force led to the destruction of all other beetle species, in the hope of creating an uber-beetle army. The challenge of doing a creature based on nature is that it is impossible to come up with a better solution than nature, so I anthropomorphized. I did a few graphite studies *à la* Scott Robertson's ant ships on some 9 x 12-inch layout paper. Iain McCaig just so happened to be in class and gave me the critique of "Fear of the Edge of the Paper," which meant my designs were all resulting in stumped and shortened servants due to the edge of my paper. He said the goddess should be tall and overpowering. It's easy to simply slip a piece of paper underneath to "add canvas." Her color palette is based on Nazi military colors.

JUSTIN PICHETRUNGSI

SEXY MARTIANS

Justin: The short-and-sweet version of my brief for this project was to design a sexy alien. The backstory is that the human race is desperate to seed onto Mars. By planting "human DNA pods" on Mars, scientists would rapidly evolve these human platforms to have the necessary traits to survive in radioactive and cosmic conditions. To design an alien is hard enough because it is key to make it relatable, which means making it more human. And now to make the alien sexy means to make her human-sexy. At the top are my first attempts. She remained a human actor with a facemask on. Bottom left, I think I hit upon something interesting.

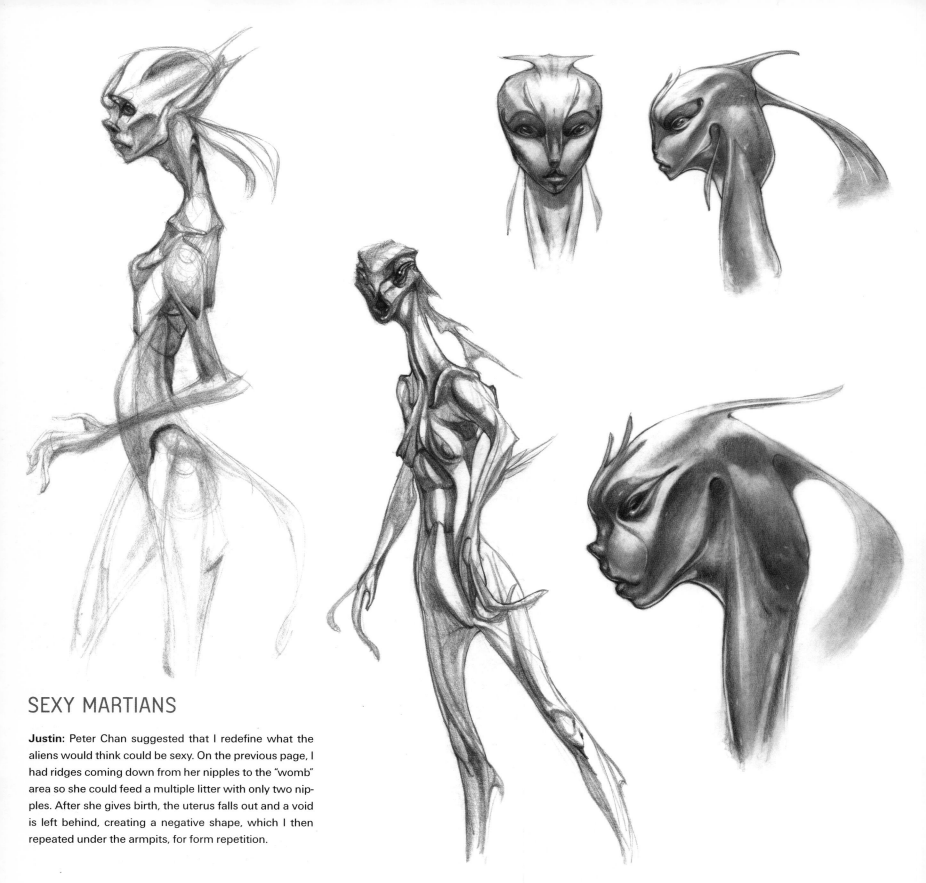

SEXY MARTIANS

Justin: Peter Chan suggested that I redefine what the aliens would think could be sexy. On the previous page, I had ridges coming down from her nipples to the "womb" area so she could feed a multiple litter with only two nipples. After she gives birth, the uterus falls out and a void is left behind, creating a negative shape, which I then repeated under the armpits, for form repetition.

FINAL DESIGN

The void would be able to be seen from a long distance, and would also serve as a protective crib for the new-born. The negative shape would be what is sexy to the aliens: representing the success of genes passed on to the next generation. Over time, the negative space would be replaced by a semi-translucent membrane.

Justin: Above is the final design. Mars has an atmosphere that is very thin, allowing more radiation and cosmic rays to enter the environment. Her "ponytail" is actually an SPF 500 shield against harmful rays for vital organs and for her baby. The "eyebrows" are smaller versions of the same organ, protecting her eyes. Her cerebellum and brainstem are larger than those of a human because of her species' increased ability of motor function and greatly developed respiratory and circulatory systems. These sketches were a lot of fun. The graphite allowed me to "sculpt" complex forms, pushing and pulling the lights and darks.

BOAR CREATURE

Marcus: These boar head studies were very fun to do. This creature was designed to be a boss in a game. The fact that his method of attack was to rush the hero with his tusks made them a key component of the design. I wanted the tusks to be a first read in the silhouette of the character's head. Some of the tusks are put in strange areas and would probably do more damage to the character than the hero, but these are exploratory sketches. I tried to have fun and give these guys an interesting attitude and aesthetic.

MANIMAL

Marcus: This disturbing creature is a "manimal." A portion of this creature is man and the other part is a mixture of feline and canine. The mixture is never 50/50. Keeping the percentage around 70/30 works fairly well and isn't as obvious. I wanted to create a rather gross animal that lived in a humid environment and was carnivorous, feeding mostly on rodents and fish. It was helpful to first look at both human and quadruped anatomy and examine the differences and similarities. I used the information I gathered to sketch the muscle structure and then stretched skin over it. Given the decision of the swamp-like environment I wanted the manimal to inhabit, I gave it short slick hair and a large snout for keen smelling ability.

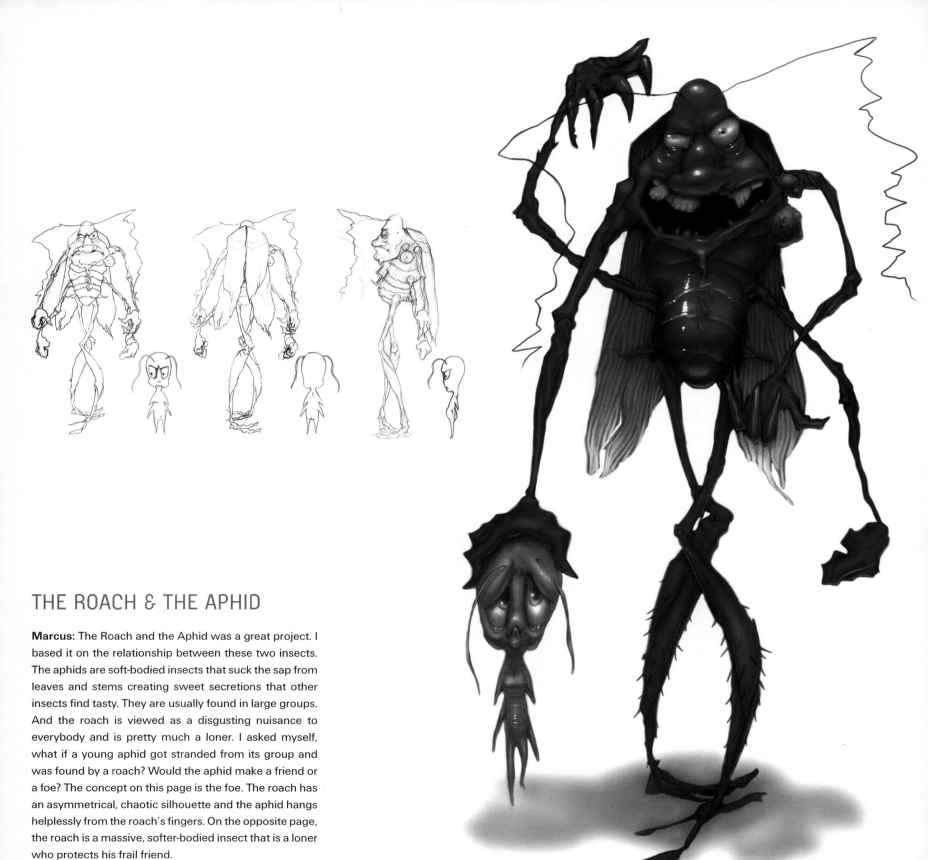

THE ROACH & THE APHID

Marcus: The Roach and the Aphid was a great project. I based it on the relationship between these two insects. The aphids are soft-bodied insects that suck the sap from leaves and stems creating sweet secretions that other insects find tasty. They are usually found in large groups. And the roach is viewed as a disgusting nuisance to everybody and is pretty much a loner. I asked myself, what if a young aphid got stranded from its group and was found by a roach? Would the aphid make a friend or a foe? The concept on this page is the foe. The roach has an asymmetrical, chaotic silhouette and the aphid hangs helplessly from the roach's fingers. On the opposite page, the roach is a massive, softer-bodied insect that is a loner who protects his frail friend.

MARCUS COLLINS

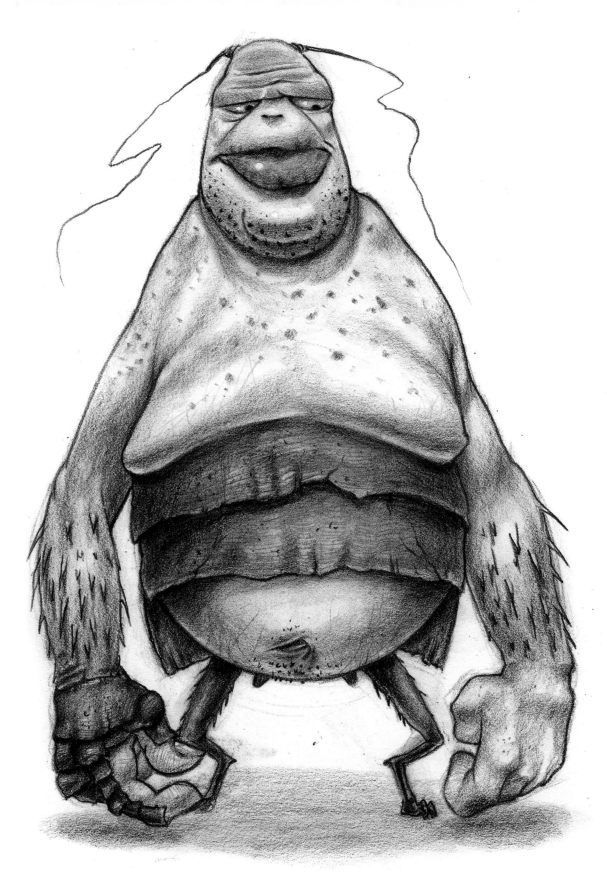

MARCUS COLLINS

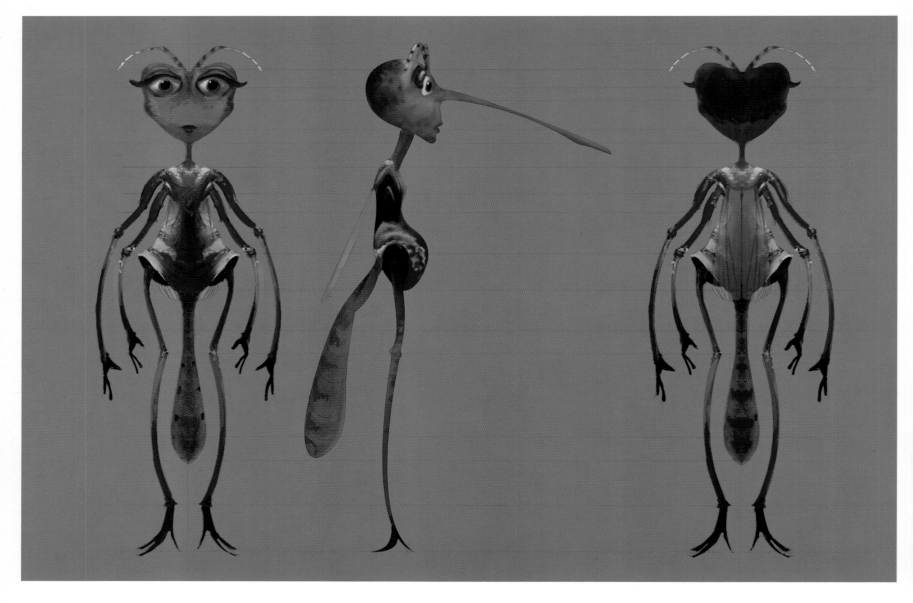

MISS MOSQUITO GARBO

Craig: Inspired by the old silent films from the early 20th century I designed a female mosquito for a short animation. While working out the design, I felt it would be best to create a quick turnaround and color study so I could better understand her. This is a fantastic way to get intimate with the design and force myself to understand the complete form. Although seemingly tedious, it's rather empowering since I have control of the design all the way up to where I would hand it off to a modeler. Once I've established the design, I can confidently position her in a painted shot that describes my intent.

CRAIG SHOJI

LEVIATHAN

Marcus: There are several definitions for Leviathan but in the broadest of terms it means a great sea monster. I wanted to explore the realms of both sea mammal and tropical fish. In my first sketch above, I referenced elephant seals and other mammals that spend their time in and out of the water. There is something about a vague, human resemblance that is really creepy, so I just had to incorporate limbs on the torso. My second approach was to create something beautiful but dangerous like the poisonous lionfish found in coral reefs. The more tropical leviathan to the left uses large colorful appendages to frighten anyone invading its space. There is no need for eyes because it feels its way around and has a strong sense of smell.

MARCUS COLLINS

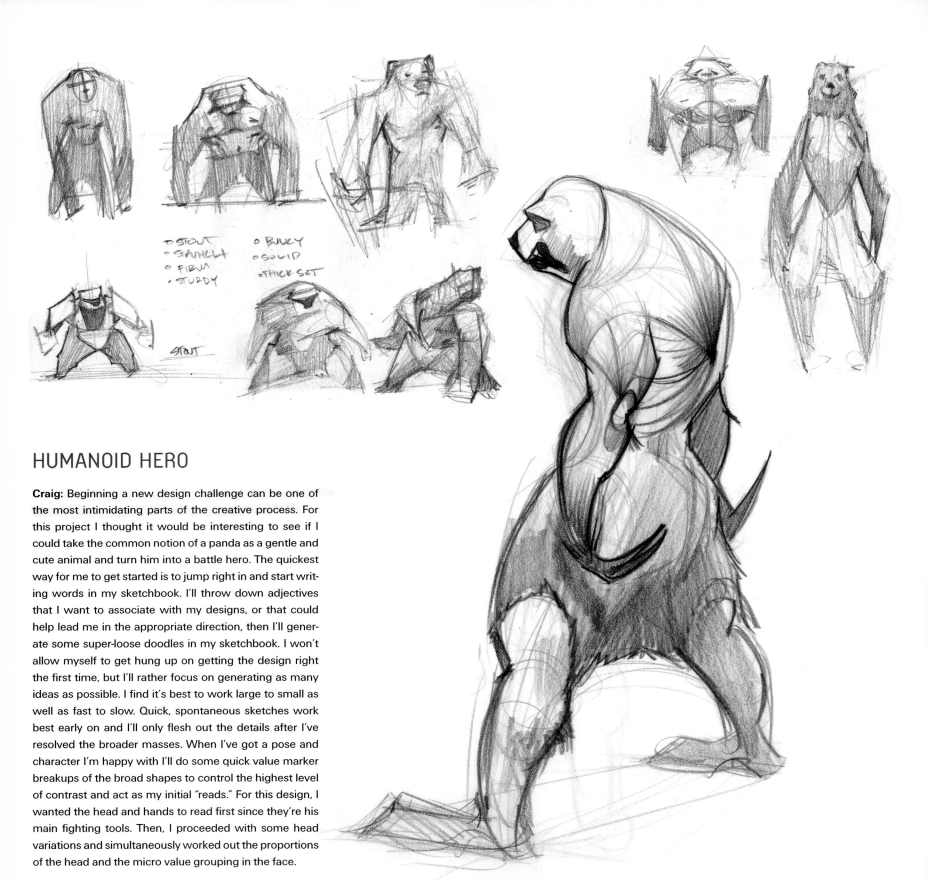

HUMANOID HERO

Craig: Beginning a new design challenge can be one of the most intimidating parts of the creative process. For this project I thought it would be interesting to see if I could take the common notion of a panda as a gentle and cute animal and turn him into a battle hero. The quickest way for me to get started is to jump right in and start writing words in my sketchbook. I'll throw down adjectives that I want to associate with my designs, or that could help lead me in the appropriate direction, then I'll generate some super-loose doodles in my sketchbook. I won't allow myself to get hung up on getting the design right the first time, but I'll rather focus on generating as many ideas as possible. I find it's best to work large to small as well as fast to slow. Quick, spontaneous sketches work best early on and I'll only flesh out the details after I've resolved the broader masses. When I've got a pose and character I'm happy with I'll do some quick value marker breakups of the broad shapes to control the highest level of contrast and act as my initial "reads." For this design, I wanted the head and hands to read first since they're his main fighting tools. Then, I proceeded with some head variations and simultaneously worked out the proportions of the head and the micro value grouping in the face.

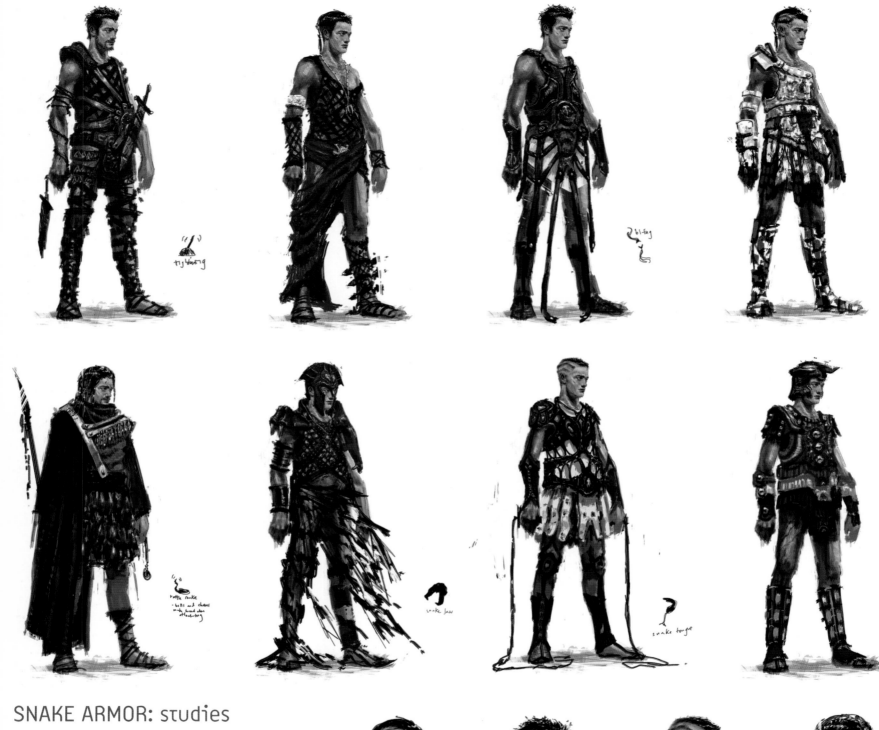

SNAKE ARMOR: studies

Peter: My main inspiration for these costume designs came from snakes. I was thinking about their characteristics such as having scaly skins, shedding, strangling and poison to help me come up with interesting designs. The face and hairstyle combinations to the right also help me to convey the character's attitude.

PETER CHAN

SNAKE ARMOR: color

Peter: *(left)* The story's protagonist is a warrior who was unwillingly granted the ability to transform into a cobra-like creature. The hero's costume is not only serpentine but incorporates themes of constraint. I integrated "grabbing" forms while keeping in mind that they would be part of the transformation into his creature form.

(above) This costume's design revolves around the dichotomy of absorbing through sight and releasing knowledge. Through the use of her powers, this character can manipulate her surroundings subtly. Her hard surface and insect-inspired headdress represent sight, contrasting with her long, fluid dress symbolizing the "rippling" of knowledge.

MANTIS ASSASSIN

Peter: Inspired by the elegant forms of the praying mantis' exoskeleton, this graceful but deadly dancer was sent on a mission to seduce and assassinate an enemy king. Weapons concealed beneath her striking formal costume are employed to provide a most exciting climax to her performance.

PETER CHAN

PETER CHAN

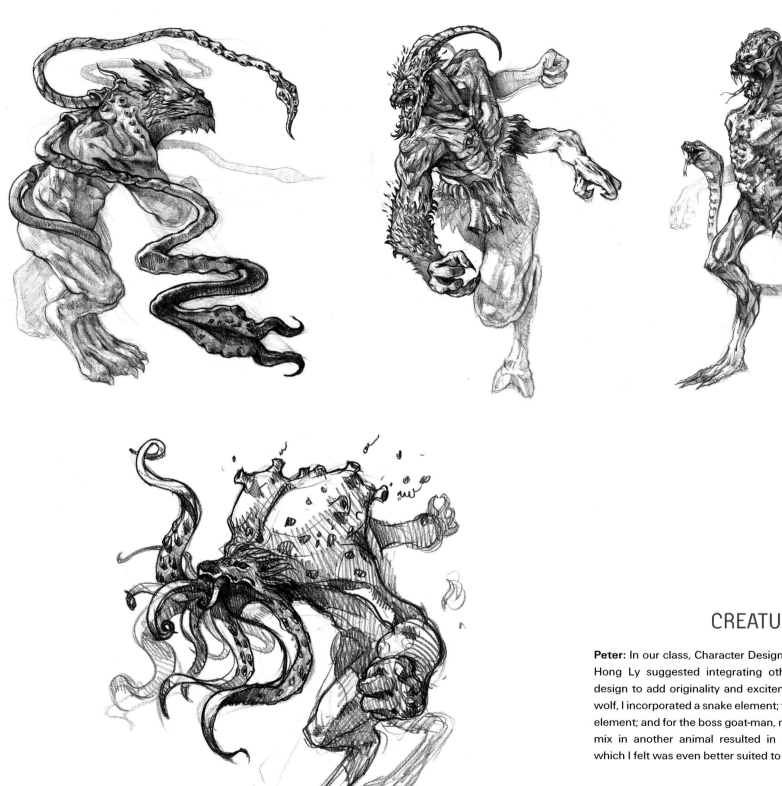

CREATURE DESIGN

Peter: In our class, Character Design 1, Kevin Chen and Hong Ly suggested integrating other animals into a design to add originality and excitement. For the were-wolf, I incorporated a snake element; for the tiger, a squid element; and for the boss goat-man, my failed attempt to mix in another animal resulted in a deformed beast, which I felt was even better suited to the character.

Richard Keyes:

Art Center's Color Theory for Entertainment is intended to be more than just the color component of a student's intellectual toolbox; it also concentrates on composition, emotional impact, adherence to story and even includes some emphasis on color for character design. Students are given a strong background in color systems, use of color palettes, the importance of light when considering color, surface effects of color, and how colors are defined by their neighbors. A majority of the class is spent on how color can help tell a story, and each class works on a different tale. Color is used to define, align and contrast characters, create atmosphere, use light instead of local color to make narrative points, and refer to some of the inherent metaphors of lighting conditions and times of day. The story you will see re-imagined in the following pages is one of the oldest in the world—the story of *Persephone*. Other classes have worked on the story of *Aladdin and the Wonderful Lamp*, *Prince Ivan and the Gray Wolf*, and H.G. Wells' *The Time Machine*.

When offered the thoroughly enjoyable job of teaching this class, I had to change tack from the way I taught illustration and graphic design students. I noticed that students who came from an industrial design background primarily used color to put warms next to cools, but also had a hunger for using color for a wider range of effects and impacts. In the attempt to respond to their zeal for more color knowledge, I think I learned as much from the class as they learned from the teacher. In 19 years of teaching I have rarely encountered such a high caliber of talent in a single group. It has been a delight to revisit these lovely images.

ABDUCTION by Justin Pichetrungsi

COOL LIGHT

Thom: This project dealt with the color differences between day lighting and twilight or night lighting, also known as sky lighting. The goal was to illustrate two different lighting conditions, warm and cool, for the same composition and subject matter. Our research involved photographing the four most common exterior lighting conditions of sky light (when the sun dips below the horizon), warm light (sunrise and sunset), noon light, and overcast lighting. Once we understood the characteristics of each, we applied the extremes of sky light and warm light to an environment of our own design. I chose this Indian palace court created for the Architectural Design 1 class.

The scene above demonstrates the condition of sky lighting, which occurs at dawn and dusk. The sky acts as an extremely diffuse blue light box evenly illuminating the environment. The excess of blue-colored light cools the local colors of all materials. In situations where light levels are low, there is a condensed range of light, lower contrast, and our perception of texture begins to become dominant. In this scene, pools of warm incandescent light emanating from lanterns interact with the warm, local colors of stone and wood to produce extremely saturated red-oranges.

WARM LIGHT

Thom: This scene demonstrates a warm lighting condition, the kind that can be observed at sunrise, sunset and late afternoon. Late afternoon, "magic hour," lighting is characterized by a naturally complimentary color palette of yellow-orange light and blue-violet shadows. The cool colors of materials such as grass, the leaves of trees, and surfaces painted blue or green become desaturated and shift toward yellow; while the warm local colors of materials such as brick, stone, and wood become warmer and much more saturated, sometimes achieving a fiery red-orange in this kind of lighting. Contrast tends to be very high. A red fringe along the border between shadow and light can sometimes be observed and lends itself to exaggera-

tion in illustration. In the example above, the red fringe of late afternoon light would not actually be visible, given the mid-afternoon sun angle that I have indicated, but I chose to exaggerate it for artistic effect.

PERSEPHONE

Thom: The story of *Persephone* from Greek mythology was the subject of these paintings. Our challenge here was to use color and lighting to set mood and reinforce the story. The most well-known part of the story, the abduction of Persephone *(top)*, describes the god of the Underworld, Hades, kidnapping Persephone from the field where she picked poppies. I imagined Hades arriving on a beast-chariot: a cadaverous bottom-feeding creature with gaping jaws and jaundiced eyes that provide the dominant color statement in the piece. Noxious smoke pours from the chariot, tinting the sky and blocking the sunlight in places. His minions in the shadows block escape and stealthily approach to seize her for their master. Some versions of the myth indicate the Underworld not as literally underground, but as a place in the east, where the souls of the dead go. The Underworld depicted here *(opposite bot-*

tom) is not underground but rather a dead marsh, an oppressive, damp, molding environment populated with large fungal stalks. The painting illustrates the moment when Hermes comes to retrieve Persephone and remove her from the Underworld. He calls to her from an acidic green field dotted with purple mushrooms, an analogue to the red poppies of her homeland.

PERSEPHONE

Thom: Persephone's mother, Demeter, wandered the earth in grief, torch in hand, searching for her daughter. I imagined that her travels would take her to many strange places far from Mount Olympus. This sketch depicts one of the many alien cities that she encountered. Foreign people, animals, and architecture were inspired by the endless variety of shapes found in the vegetable world, *i.e.,* beans, peas, peppers, onions, radishes, gourds, etc. This image began as a small thumbnail sketch and quick digital comp to test the lighting and mood against the story point being illustrated. The placement of the largest shapes, color, and depth were set very quickly, which helped to justify proceeding to the next stage in which time was spent adding details, rendering and creating the finished piece above.

ROOM WITH A RIVER VIEW

Justin: I wanted Hades to be a compassionate character, kidnapping Persephone only to prove something to her, not for love or lust. Hades' palace is designed after a pitcher plant, a carnivorous plant that captures its prey by luring them into a sweet but ultimately rotting venue. The floating River of Styx is a river of souls and worthless bodies—each one representing the bad deeds of mankind. I had a blurry image in my mind of the beginning of *Schindler's List*. Hades opens the bedroom curtains to Persephone and says, "Look at the rot, what a view." Disgusted, he continues, "This is what I have to live with. Mankind has sins, which you Olympians refuse to see. Life is not perfect. People are not perfect and not all good. Know this." Our rescuer, Hermes, is in the foreground.

JUSTIN PICHETRUNGSI

LOOKING BACK

Justin: This was a more modern concept of Hades. Hermes takes one last look back as he descends down the stairs of the greasy, grimy Underworld. This started out a 1 x 2-inch graphite sketch taken to "speedpaint" level.

Scott Robertson:

Location, location, location. You have heard it before and we all know how important it is for where you choose to live and work. And as it turns out, location is also one of the most important things in conveying the proper setting to tell a story. To this point we have examples from two of the classes being taught in the program, Architectural Design 1 and 2.

Architectural Design 1 trains students to draw and design buildings from many different architectural periods and genres. With the focus on exterior design, the students are presented with the archetypes of about fifteen different architectural styles throughout the 14-week term. Each week they are asked to research and draw buildings from these differing genres. In addition to drawing existing buildings from various time periods in order to develop their visual libraries, they are asked to infuse each with some original design intent of their own. By enhancing the architecture this way, it becomes better suited to the telling of a story, and thus increases its entertainment value. A good working target for "real" or "historic" versus "imagined" architecture is about a 70/30 split. A successful execution of this will be subtle and should not be the first thing a casual viewer of the work is drawn to. First and foremost, the exterior of the building being designed should be in keeping with the architectural genre assigned for that week. Only upon closer inspection should the viewer sense the enhanced reality or originality of the design. All of the decisions made in the design of the building should be done to support the genre assigned and then, the story being told.

Architectural Design 2 moves from the exterior of the building to the interior. During this class the students are asked to design two interior environments from a list of three choices. The interior types were: monumental as in a large museum, a dwelling, or a video-game level with at least five different rooms. The stories they create, which take place in their designed interiors, must be of very different time periods. What you will see throughout the chapter is a wide range of styles and designs. Many of the finely executed perspective drawings seen throughout this chapter were also worked on in the Advanced Perspective drawing class.

In the big picture of entertainment design, the creation of the environments can and should be a key component to supporting the storytelling. All too often character-specific designers forget that having the ability to draw and illustrate their characters or hero vehicles in the proper environment can go a long way toward communicating even more about their design. In addition to providing the backdrop for the characters and vehicles to move through, the environment itself can become the focal point and one of the main "characters" of a story. In the coming school terms, the students will be placing greater emphasis on their ability to render more dramatic atmospheric and lighting conditions within their environments.

Again, the focus of this chapter is Architectural Design 1 and 2, with the examples demonstrating our introduction of how to design, draw and render various architectural exteriors and interiors. At this point in the program, these assignments are more for the purpose of building the students' visual library than of telling a specific story.

Gary Meyer:

In the Architectural Design Classes 1 and 2, I was pleased to be involved with students who not only created interesting stories but were able to express them well, with good perspective, color and dynamic design.

THE CLEANERS by Jonathan Bach

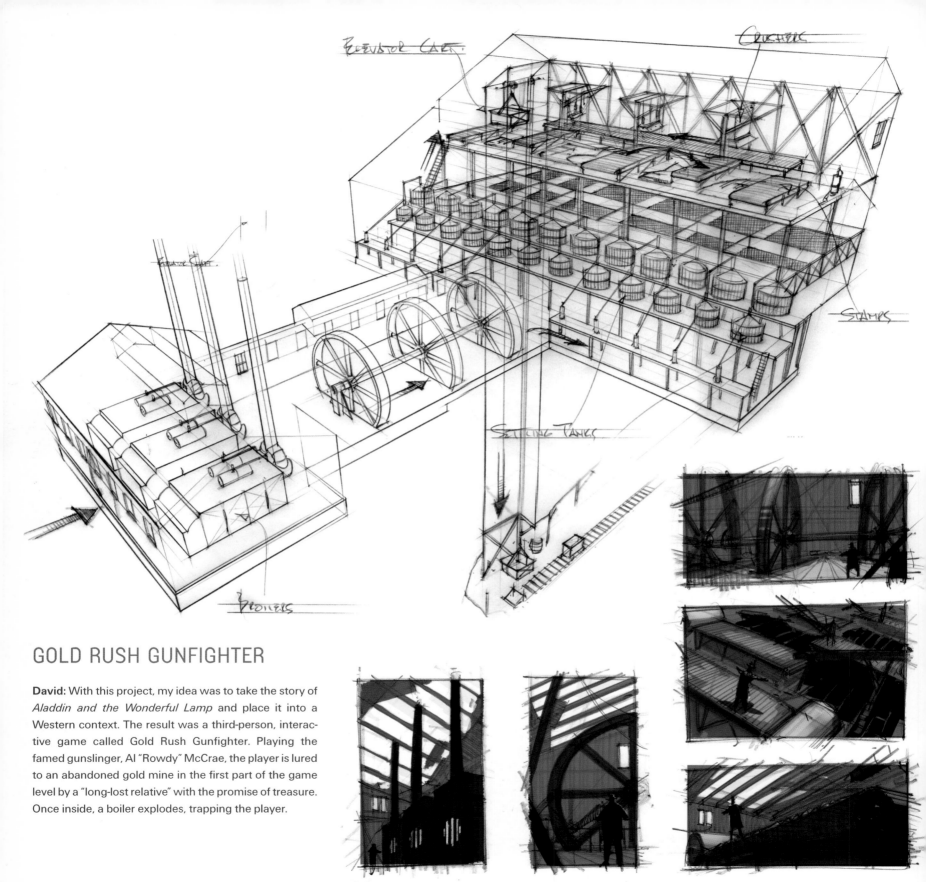

Labels on the technical drawing: ELEVATOR CAGE, CRUSHERS, ELEVATOR SHAFT, STAMPS, SETTLING TANKS, BROILERS

GOLD RUSH GUNFIGHTER

David: With this project, my idea was to take the story of *Aladdin and the Wonderful Lamp* and place it into a Western context. The result was a third-person, interactive game called Gold Rush Gunfighter. Playing the famed gunslinger, Al "Rowdy" McCrae, the player is lured to an abandoned gold mine in the first part of the game level by a "long-lost relative" with the promise of treasure. Once inside, a boiler explodes, trapping the player.

DAVID HOBBINS

GOLD RUSH GUNFIGHTER

David: He or she must successfully navigate this dangerous environment of enormous spinning cogwheels, conveyor belts and crushing machines while fending off grizzly bears and American Indian ghouls. Placing an emphasis on story and gameplay, I wanted the action largely to dictate the level design, but still retain some functionality. After exploration through many thumbnails such as those on the right, I finally achieved a rough sketch that described the level in detail so that I could pursue the final renderings with greater continuity.

DAVID HOBBINS

HAUNTED BATHROOM

Victoria: For the horror-survival video game I was designing, I used an ordinary place to create an eerie environment. I always thought that bathrooms were a little creepy because of their coldness and the smell of stagnant water. My goal was to make the viewer question the room first, notice that there was something wrong and then see the ghost faces in the mirror.

VICTORIA YING

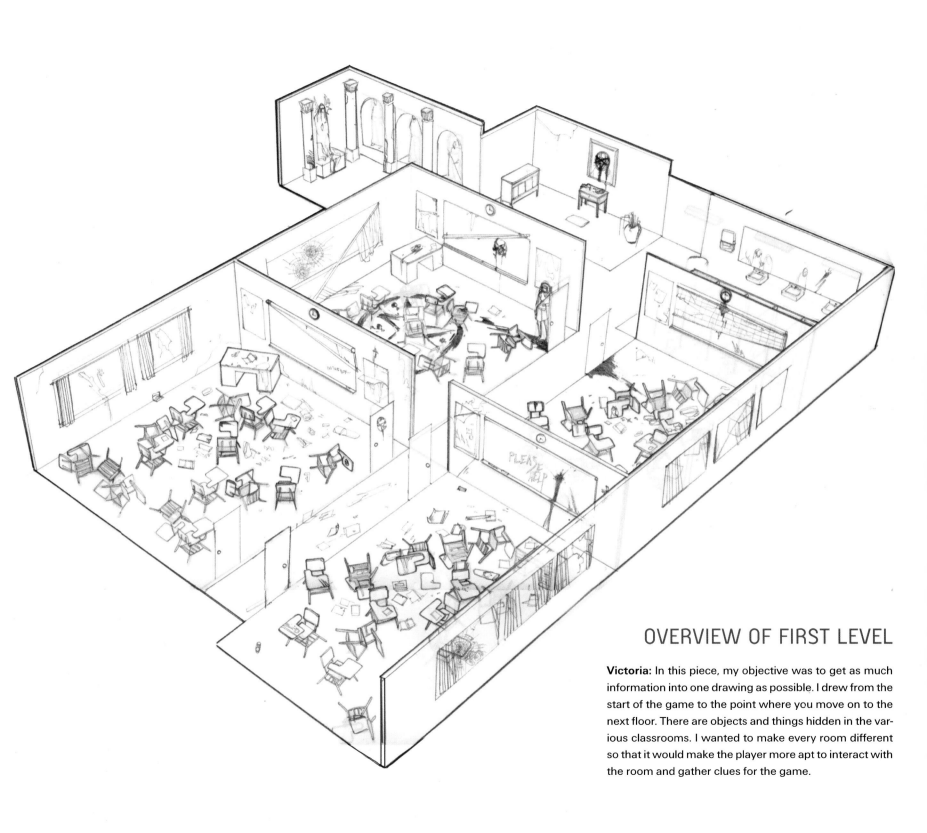

OVERVIEW OF FIRST LEVEL

Victoria: In this piece, my objective was to get as much information into one drawing as possible. I drew from the start of the game to the point where you move on to the next floor. There are objects and things hidden in the various classrooms. I wanted to make every room different so that it would make the player more apt to interact with the room and gather clues for the game.

EYE OF THE BIRD AND WORM

Simon: I sketched this down shot because it puts the viewer in a dynamic and thrilling position: very high up! I was experimenting with placing ancient architecture into foreign environments as an exercise.

On the next page, I addressed the opposite extreme view from the floor. A large interior space allows for more control over lighting, which this color study shows. The bottom observational sketches are a great way to practice line weight and build confidence, not to mention that they are just plain fun. After sketching a gothic cathedral with pen, anything seems possible.

SIMON KO

RENAISSANCE PALACE
MUGHAL TOMB

Raj: The piece to the right is an exploration of Islamic Indian Architecture. Throughout Indian history the subcontinent has experienced pilgrimage, trade and imperialism from a variety of foreign cultures. During the 16th century the Mughal Empire from the north ruled much of northern India. It is this influence that left a lasting influence on the architectural history of the subcontinent. This piece explores one of the signatures of Islamic Indian architecture, the tomb. Although the design expresses a scale much larger than reality, I wanted to create a scene of grandeur and monumentality for the travelers paying their respects.

The piece above is an example of the revival of specific architectural motifs during the Renaissance. The ideas of symmetry and rationality in design, the use of the dome and semicircular arch, and a sense of regularity in spatial divisions are explored in this design. The scale is pushed towards the monumental to give a sense of Romanesque grandiosity.

RAJ RIHAL

GNOME THUMBNAILS

Shae: This was a story about gnomes in a subterranean complex at the beginning of the 20th century. Consequently, I looked to European Art Nouveau for inspiration. In designing interiors, I start by sketching many thumbnails, eventually picking a few of them for development. Occasionally, I start to break the problem down by doing some detail drawings, taking a moment out of one sketch for closer examination.

THE ENVIRONMENT PROCESS

Hamzah: The secret to a successful environment design is research and composition. I scribbled loosely all the research I had for the Hindu/Thailand/Cambodia theme with big shapes until I had a composition that I was satisfied with. Then I went in and detailed out the shapes using the found research as a guide. I liked the image of the jungle ruin in Cambodia so I started with the tree roots tangled on a statue bust and worked outward from there. The rest of the piece was up to happy accidents and the imagination they bring about. This process is the best working method for me. To bring a level of closure to the piece, I outlined shapes and objects that I felt needed to be popped forward while leaving the rest of the image receding away into space.

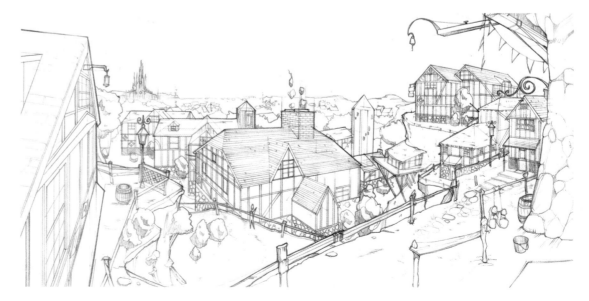

HAMZAH KASOM

WORKING LOOSELY

Hamzah: On the left is a typical thumbnail I would produce. Using a Pilot Hi-Tec C pen and a lot of elbow grease, I work loosely, keeping in mind that it's only a thumbnail and nothing more. I like using a pen because it forces me to accept any accident produced, to keep going forward and not look back at my mistakes; I work faster this way and generate more results. I can probably take this thumbnail and jump straight into the painting, but I usually like to figure out every little detail first. The top image is an example of a more finished piece I would use before throwing colors into it. Once I am satisfied with my thumbnail, I scan, resize, and print it in a lower opacity to draw over; keeping the freshness of the sketch and cleaning it up with a bolder drawing.

HAMZAH KASOM

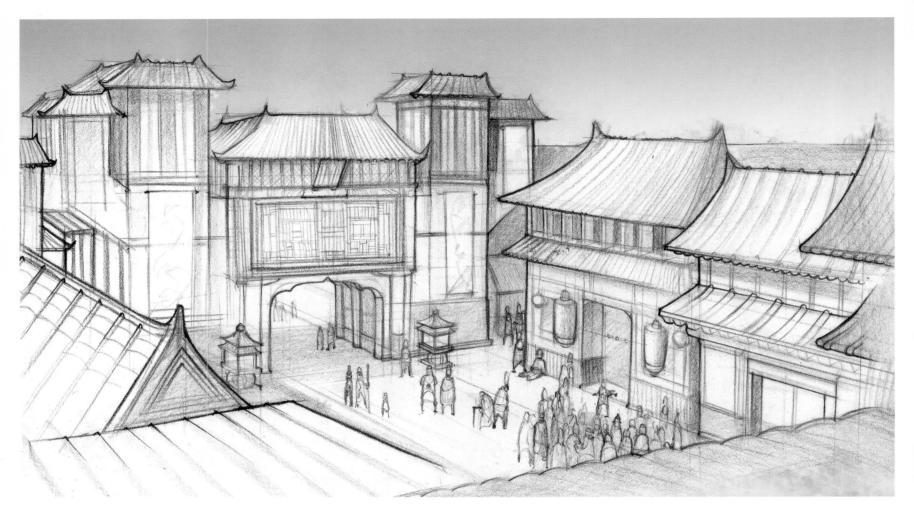

ORIENTAL MARKET | MEDIEVAL BAZAAR

Eric: I wanted to provide an interesting point of view while utilizing reference to make the drawing believable. The viewer is given a glimpse of the city from the rooftop. This piece reflects the design of the Tang Dynasty such as the roof curls with a fishtail-like design motif. These types of pencil sketches allow me to quickly draw an underlay, which I can further develop with darker pencil work. The final step is to darken the edges in order to pull out the forms contained in the overlapping shapes of my design.

I enjoyed designing in the Tudor architectural style because I found it interesting that the houses tended to have smaller footprints than their bodies. In this sketch, I show the houses aligned onto a grid only to be divided by the cobblestone pathways to the church.

ERIC NG

RENAISSANCE RENDEZVOUS

In my research, I learned that while many Tudor houses resembled each other and looked similar, they differed in the design and placement of the trim. I utilized this to create an environment that had uniqueness even though there was repeating architecture.

Eric: I found that in Renaissance architecture, architects used many curves within their designs. On their walls and buildings, they had layers and layers of designs that built one on top of the other. This piece was designed as a courtyard where a messenger was to meet with the duke behind the fountain.

LAB DISECTIKA | PETROGRAD HOME 1918

Craig: Once I have an idea in mind for a space, I'll flesh it out with a high-angle line drawing like the one on the right. This allows me to get a better feel for where objects sit in that space, and how a character would navigate through the area. Then I'll do some compositional sketches to determine the best immersive camera position to describe the shot. When I feel I've got a drawing with potential, I'll do a quick marker sketch of it to determine the value grouping and key lighting. The two sketches on the facing page were my conceptualization for the interior of a home in Petrograd following the Russian revolution of 1917. The top image illustrates the drawing room where a tenant has set up her bed close to a small warming stove. The lower image is a bathroom that is communally shared and doubles as a washbasin for the dishes. Once the lighting is established, I'll make a color comp and then a rendered painting. The final painting illustrates the mood, color key, and lighting of the space. This particular final, above, is from a separate project and is a shot of a containment lab for storing and dissecting creatures.

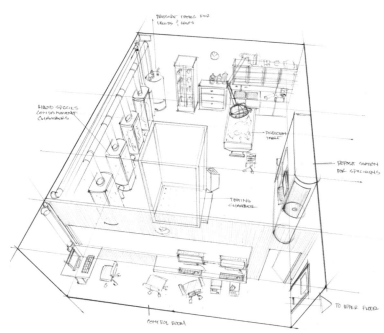

CRAIG SHOJI

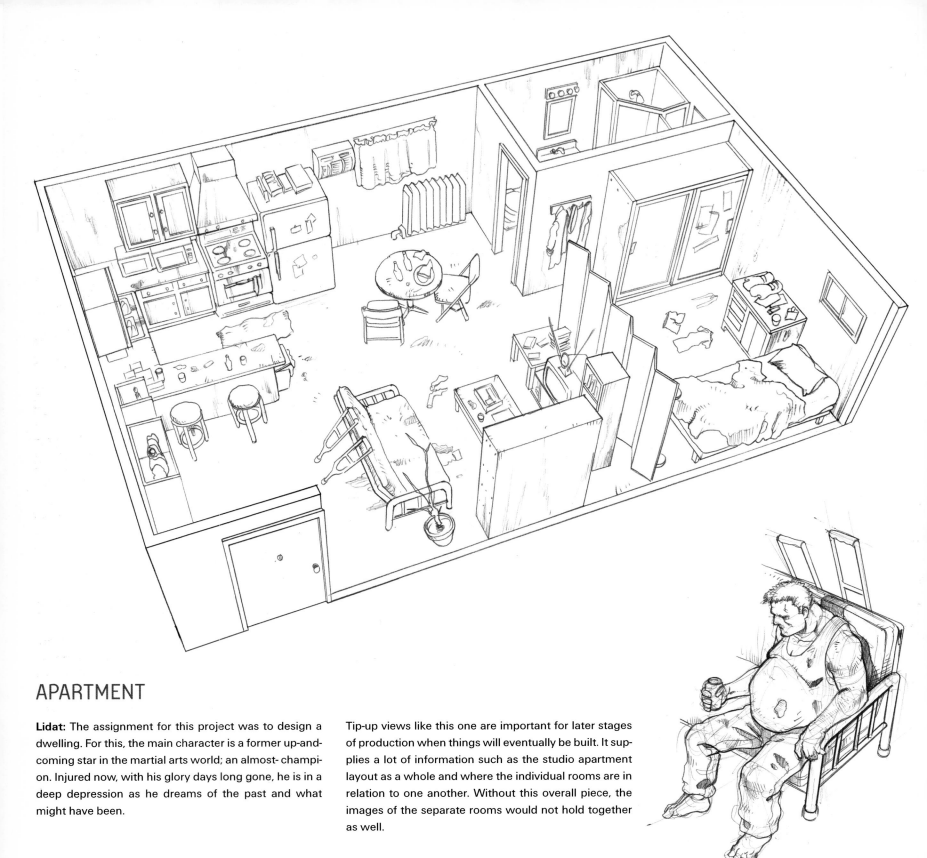

APARTMENT

Lidat: The assignment for this project was to design a dwelling. For this, the main character is a former up-and-coming star in the martial arts world; an almost- champion. Injured now, with his glory days long gone, he is in a deep depression as he dreams of the past and what might have been.

Tip-up views like this one are important for later stages of production when things will eventually be built. It supplies a lot of information such as the studio apartment layout as a whole and where the individual rooms are in relation to one another. Without this overall piece, the images of the separate rooms would not hold together as well.

LIDAT TRUONG

KITCHEN & BEDROOM

Lidat: Here I am trying to show the character's depressive state through his run-down kitchen and bedroom. Everything is worn, stained and covered in grime. The sink is filled with long-unwashed dishes and the table and counters are littered with empty beer bottles and cans. Clothes are strewn about the bedroom floor. By his bed are a glass and bottle of alcohol suggesting he drinks often to drown his misery. Hanging from the wall are his old training *gi* and belt. On the nightstand by his bed are his old sparring gloves. He can't bring himself to pack them away and leave behind that part of his life.

BATHROOM & ENTRANCE

Lidat: Just like the rest of the apartment, these areas are also in a state of disrepair. The bathroom is covered with stains, the linoleum floor is bubbling and peeling, and one of the light bulbs is out. At the entrance of the apartment is a case housing his old competition *gi* and a trophy shelf, which are polished and clean. They are the only things in the whole apartment that are kept in good shape. Their pristine condition contrasts with everything around them, drawing attention to the fact that he longs for and lives in the past.

SPIDER PALACE

Peter: The spider palace was designed to be a game level where the character fights giant spiders. My original idea, as illustrated in the sketch to the left, was to have the spiders camouflaged as plants and have them crawl out from the giant pots. I later thought it would be more interesting visually and gameplay-wise, if the spider was physically connected to the pot and used it for attack.

PETER CHAN

ZOMBIE MORGUE

Peter: This piece is the beginning stage for my game level design. I was inspired by Chinese zombie movies that I grew up watching. I took advantage of various props that are associated with Chinese zombies to make the environment more exotic.

PETER CHAN

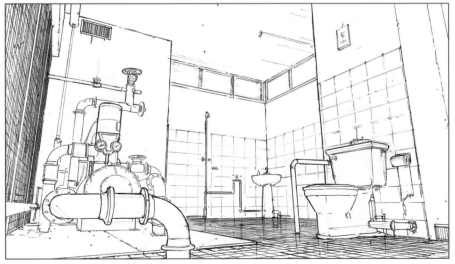

THE ABANDONED: bathroom

Peter: This is one of three rooms I designed for the interior dwelling project. The story is about an obsessed doctor that converted an abandoned hospital into his living quarters. The steam coming out from the boiler and the cast shadow of the figure helps to make it feel much more mysterious than a regular bathroom.

PETER CHAN

PETER CHAN

THE ABANDONED: kitchen

Peter: This is an autopsy room converted into the doctor's kitchen. I thought the body freezer would be perfect as his refrigerator where he keeps food and his favorite preservatives. Most of my time was spent developing the thumbnails on the facing page to find the best viewing angle for this image.

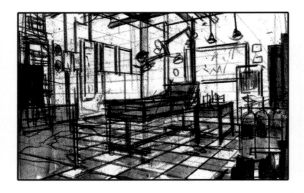

PETER CHAN

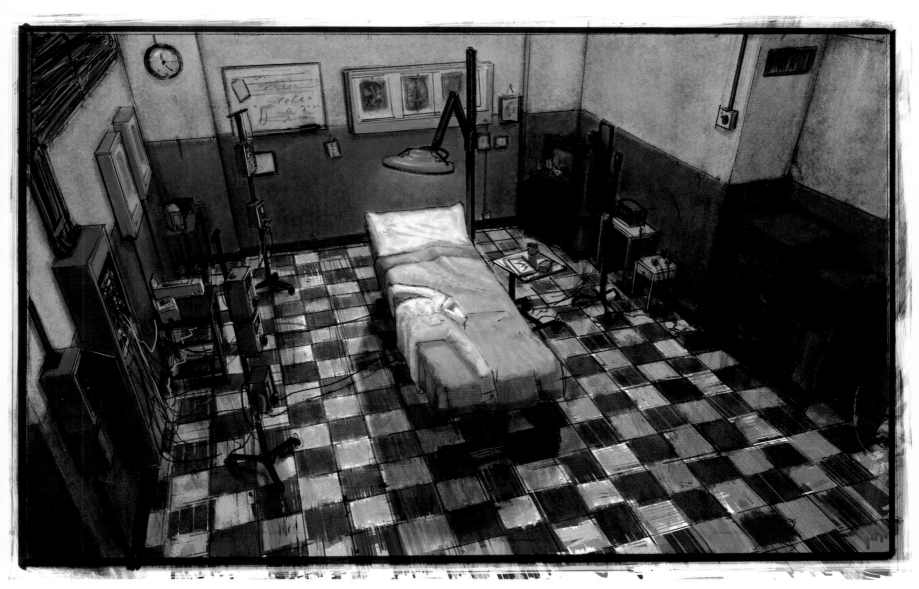

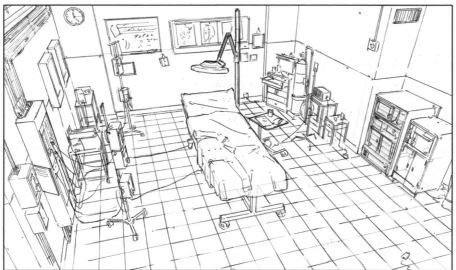

THE ABANDONED: bedroom

Peter: The surgery room is converted into his bedroom. I like the idea of the room being the human body and using the medical equipment as a metaphor for the organs. The colored wires on the floor also help to suggest veins and nerves. The doctor has decorated his room with his favorite X-rays.

RIVAL GODS

Jonathan: The designs on these two pages are for an adventure game based loosely on Aztec mythology. There were two rival gods: Huitzilopochtli, the Aztec god of war, and Quetzalcoatl, the god of life. In the game each god wants to renew the world in a drastic and devastating way, but the player does not know which one is actually fighting on the side of mankind. The two main characters are a storied warrior who is a survivor of a devastated Aztec state and a seemingly insane priest, systematically sacrificing his way through the whole of the Aztec world. Each is backed by a god respectively. They must fight each other using what resources they have at their disposal to prevail. The player will choose which side he wants to support in the end and only then will he know if the right decision has been made.

JONATHAN BACH

RIVAL GODS

Jonathan: These four pieces focus on the bone altar: the last level of the game. The largest image shows the final, hopeless moment when the warrior Tula meets Quetzalcoatl. He is nothing but a speck in the face of the awesome power of Quetzalcoatl, until Huitzilopochtli endows him with his own fierce strength. I put the focus on scale in these pieces by showing everything at extreme angles with a wide-angle lens.

THE CLEANERS

Jonathan: In a crashing Japanese economy, a community of kids in a suburb has been left orphaned by parents unable to handle financial ruin. With all but the cruelest adults out of the picture, the children have formed gangs for profit and protection. One such group of kids finds refuge in an abandoned cleaners and it becomes home to their strange, new family. They must fend for themselves by stealing and selling wares while escaping the dangers of exploitation by adults and older gangs of kids. They use their creativity and ingenuity to make the cleaners a livable and even enjoyable home.

JONATHAN BACH

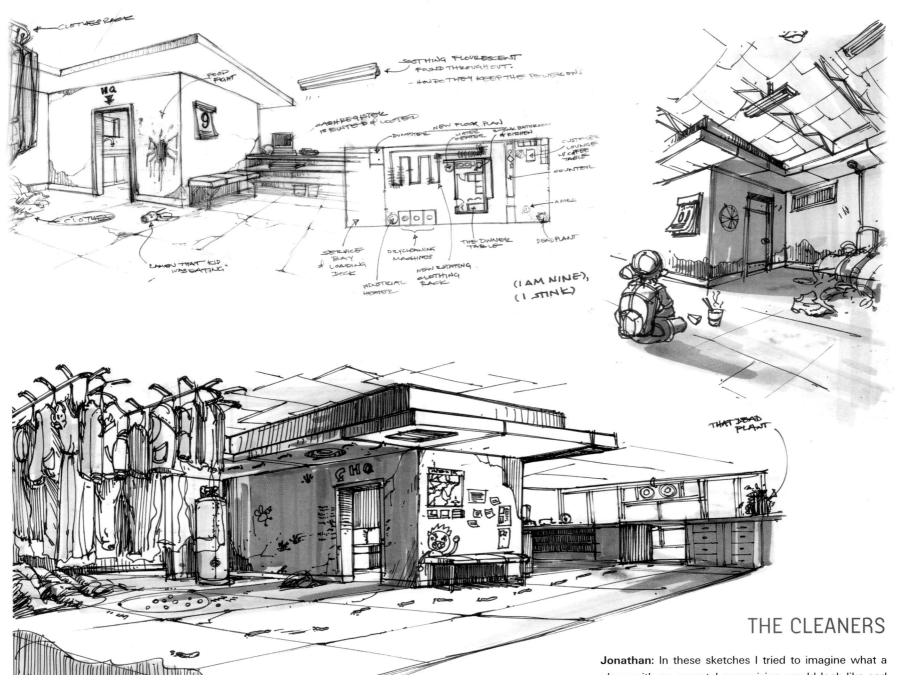

The following labels appear on the sketches:

CLOTHES RACK

SOOTHING FLOURESCENT FOUND THROUGHOUT.
– HOW DO THEY KEEP THE POWER ON?

FOOD FIGHT

HQ

9

CASH REGISTER IS BUSTED & LOOTED

NEW FLOOR PLAN

DUMPSTER   WATER HEATER   2-SINK BATHROOM & KITCHEN

CUSTOMER LOUNGE & CAFE TABLE

COUNTER

A MELL

CLOTHES

RAMEN THAT KID WAS EATING

SERVICE BAY & LOADING DOCK

DRYCLEANING MACHINES

INDUSTRIAL HEATER

NEW ROTATING CLOTHING RACK

THE DINNER TABLE

DEAD PLANT

(I AM NINE), (I STINK)

THAT IS BAD PLANT

GHQ

THE CLEANERS

Jonathan: In these sketches I tried to imagine what a place with no parental supervision would look like and even smell like. I imagined the whole building would be used for childhood games, which were never cleaned up or even finished. The kids would leave their messes and as a result there would be piles of clothes used in tent-building rituals and loose refuse from sporadic meals. Even though the story of how the children came together was dark, I tried to keep things playful by showing things through the perspective of the children whose resilience would have them forgetting about the bad times by making light of their situation at every chance possible.

THE CLEANERS

Jonathan: Upstairs, where the previous owner used to live, the children have made a comfortable—though not hygienic—dwelling. The kids are becoming quite the graffiti artists. They practice often on the walls. It wasn't hard for me to indicate that the kids were inexperienced at graffiti because it was my first time writing. In addition to my own attempts at the art, I enlisted the help of my two friends Justin Pichetrungsi and Craig Shoji, the two hardest street taggers I know. In all the images from The Cleaners project, my goal was to show activity, traffic, and playfulness.

JONATHAN BACH

THE CLEANERS

Jonathan: I've seen dirtier. Even so, I think that I'd have a hard time walking into this one. On a trip to Japan I had the experience of using a squatting stall at an airport, among other places. I guess this style of toilet just says "Japan" to me; I had to include it in the project. Just like everything else, going to the bathroom is a game to kids. To the right of the stall I drew some test cups where the kids had labeled their samples and waited patiently to see what would grow. A little gross you say? Not to 12 preteen boys.

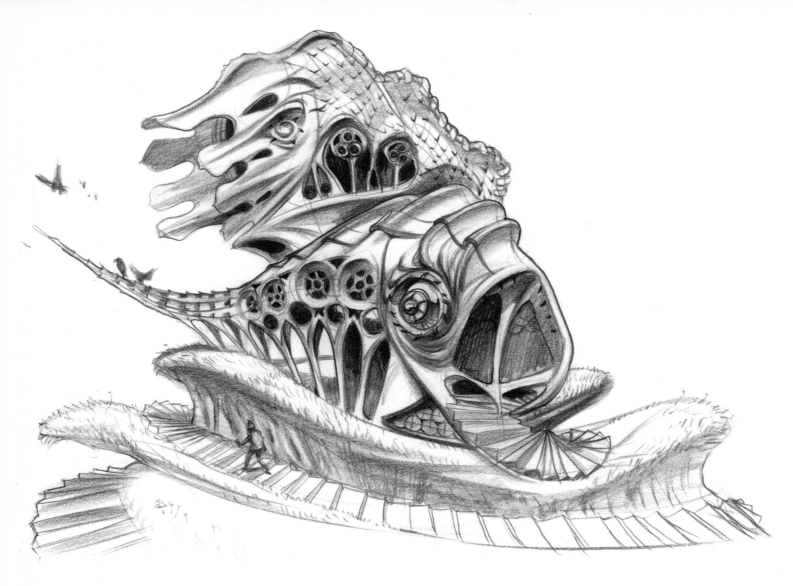

GAUDI & ORIENTAL BUILDINGS

Justin: In the top piece, my goal was to fuse gesture, a principle not common to architecture, with sculptural forms influenced by Antoni Gaudi. The concept of the piece was to have two fish splashing out of the ground to create the home of an eccentric alchemist. In designing period architecture, like the oriental pieces to the right, it is important to ask oneself how would I do it differently if I were an architect of the time? Some easy ways of redesigning any existing design is changing scale, location, technology or physics-based restraints. Another important point is to have a clear focus on what you want that piece to be about, be it the ginormous scale and depth, or the verticality of the city.

JUSTIN PICHETRUNGSI

JUSTIN PICHETRUNGSI

ORIGIN OF SPECIES

Justin: These pieces were done for a story I developed called "Origin of Species," which is an adaptation of the journey of Charles Darwin to the Galapagos Islands. Upon arriving at the islands on the *H.M.S. Beagle*, Darwin realizes the secret of this enchanted land where the wildlife and even the natives have evolved to a far superior level. After befriending the natives for a few days, he comes back to his partially sunken and abandoned ship. His investigation leads him to believe that the ship was recognized as an evolutionary threat and sunk by the coral as a defense maneuver. Having most of the *Beagle* at his disposal, he makes the best of what he has, converting the crew's quarters to a greenhouse, making his own aviary, and having areas to store and conduct experiments.

JUSTIN PICHETRUNGSI

GREENHOUSE

Justin: On the left page, I had a lot of fun set-dressing Darwin's study. I researched what his study looked like at home and translated that to his sea-study. I found the exact two microscopes he owned and put one in his study and the other in the greenhouse. Since this is a period piece, I did a lot of research on what the ships of that time looked like and what their structures were. It was important to make sure the props, furniture, and clothing matched with the time period. The piece to the left is an example of using a two- or three-value study to establish the focus of the composition. It is important to design the "shadow" and "light" shapes, while maintaining the true physics.

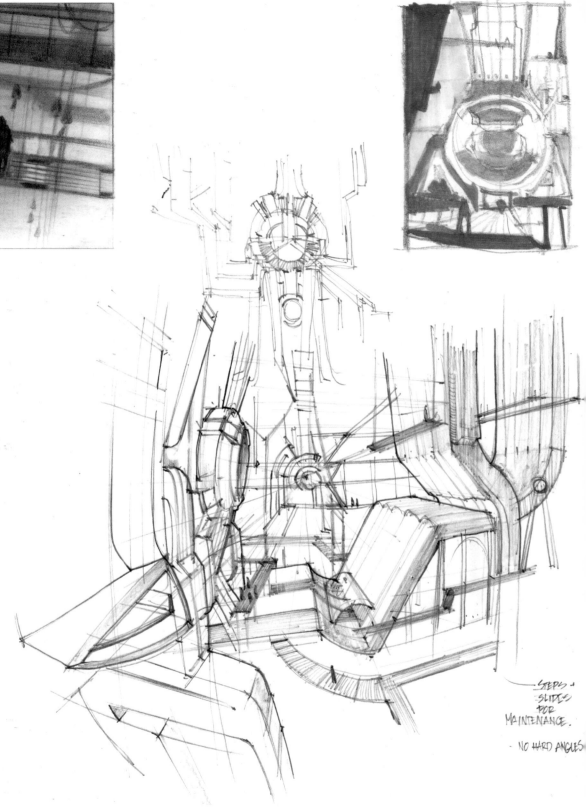

ORGAN, PIPES & SOUND

Justin: For the video game level project, I developed a story called "Staccato." The story is basically *Indiana Jones* meets *Phantom of the Opera*. It was important to me to integrate original gameplay with the design of the level. My story had to do with a secret, hidden inside an enormous organ, protected by a guardian. I decided early on that the gameplay would be dictated by sound and music. Sound would be a weapon and its only counter would be the inverse sound wave. These are comps for the backstage and auditorium, which is separated by the organ. Some of these are done with graphite and marker, or just plain graphite and moved around with a Webril pad. Opposite top right is a mix of traditional and digital media.

STEPS &
SLIDES
FOR
MAINTENANCE.

- NO HARD ANGLES

JUSTIN PICHETRUNGSI

STACCATO

Justin: To find the visual style of my architecture, I did studies of music notes and then eventually created my own calligraphy. The music calligraphy is great because it has so many dynamic "thick-to-thin" transitions. Music has its own dynamics in sound, such as *crescendo* and *decrescendo*, or *legato* and *staccato*. I incorporated the music dynamics into the graphic dynamics by making the enemy forms very sharp, short, "quick," and unconnected, while keeping the protagonist forms fluid and connected. An example of this is in the graphite sketch, on the opposite page, top right: I made the enemy troops like "staccato" notes on a music sheet.

JUSTIN PICHETRUNGSI

STAIRWELL

Justin: These are some thumbnails. The top left one was
an idea for the main stairwell.

JUSTIN PICHETRUNGSI

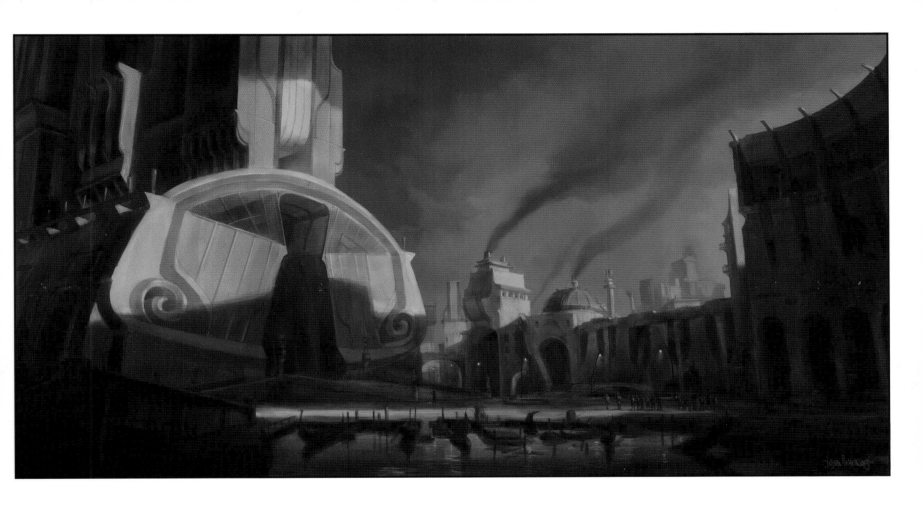

OPERA HOUSE

Justin: After I arrived at the visual style, the task was left to translate the flat abstract forms to spatial and intentional architecture. Since lighting in the opera house was important, I did my thumbnails with graphite, erasing away to create the luminous areas. The purpose of the exterior shot of the opera house was to contrast the war-torn city against the sanctuary of the opera house. An important visual cue was the five lines on music sheets, which I carried out to the exterior. It's fun to create little moments in a big piece to keep the viewer's eye moving: *e.g.,* the soldiers under the lamp, the boat's reflections on the water, or the alley with a little bridge.

JUSTIN PICHETRUNGSI

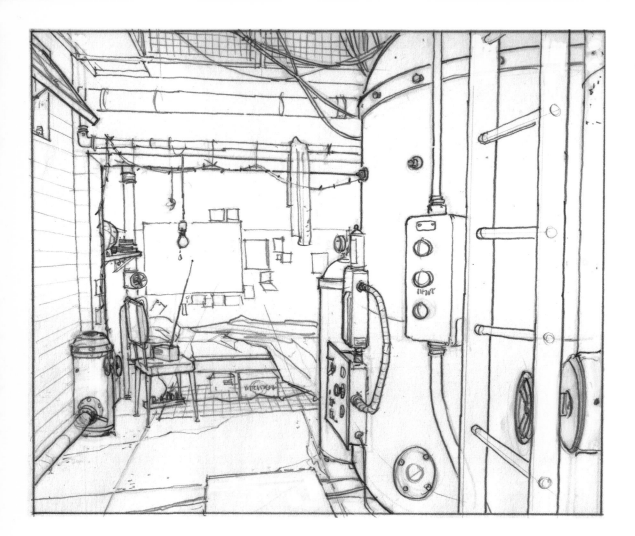

THE SUPER

Thom: These drawings represent the peculiar dwelling of "The Super," an eccentric maintenance man who has converted a decommissioned basement boiler room in the building where he works into his private residence. This character and space were inspired by some of the quirky property managers and absentee landlords that I have had the fortune to know. The space is dressed to communicate the details of this character's personality and lifestyle, such as the haphazard retrofitting of the equipment in this cramped room to facilitate showering, cooking, heating and lighting. For these sketches I quickly set up a cube, a few cylinders and a camera in a 3-D program and then screen captured four wireframe views to use as drawing underlays. For such a simple space the use of a model was not necessary, but being able to move around rough geometry in 3-D allowed me to quickly find interesting compositions from viewpoints that actually exist, given the size constraints of such a confined space. Value was added in Photoshop.

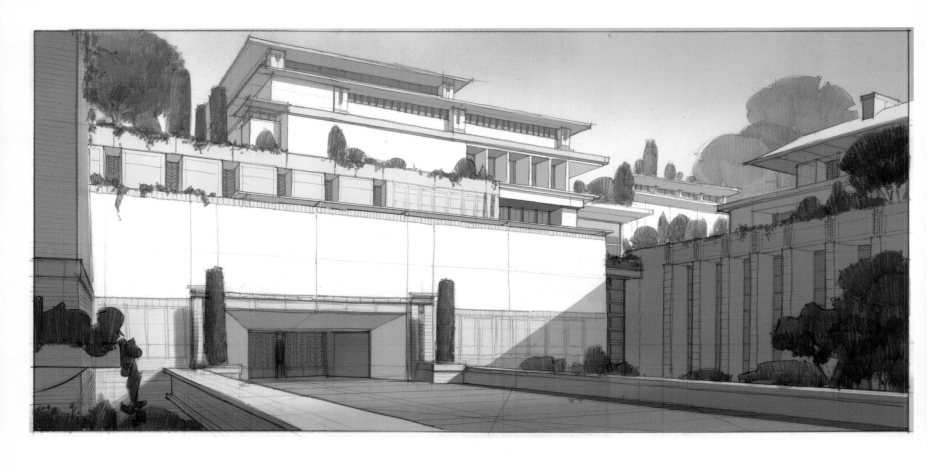

ARCHITECTURAL GENRES

Thom: This turn-of-the-century modern residence is a blend of the Prairie and Usonian styles, *à la* Frank Lloyd Wright *(top)*. Vegetation provides scale as well as ornamentation consistent with the period. A renaissance structure fronting a deserted piazza and fountain along a canal recalls a Florentine setting *(right)*. A medieval village surrounds a Romanesque church and bell tower *(opposite page, bottom left)*. Also depicted, an enormous terraced ziggurat of Babylonian construction reminiscent of Nebuchadnezzar's hanging gardens *(above right)*, and a view up the Euphrates toward a distant ziggurat of colossal scale *(opposite page, bottom right)*. While architecture of this scale would not have been possible to build at the time, given the available materials and construction methods, it is entertaining to see characteristic Babylonian design elements applied to buildings of such impossible scale. These drawings are graphite on Canson marker paper with value added digitally.

ARCHITECTURAL GENRES

Thom: This scene is immediately identifiable as a village of medieval Europe *(top)*. Characteristic of the wattle-and-daub construction method of the period, exposed timbers provide a graphically interesting pattern on building facades. The winding medieval streets are a contrast to the carefully designed space around early 20th century modern buildings *(right)*. I especially admire the elaborate decorative motifs and variety of shapes found in Indian and Islamic architecture *(opposite page, top)*. This Indian palace blends elements of the Buddhist, Hindu, and Islamic traditions. A Romanesque basilica and a Neo-Classical château *(opposite page, bottom)* both rely on classical shapes and proportions. These drawings are graphite on Canson marker paper with value added digitally.

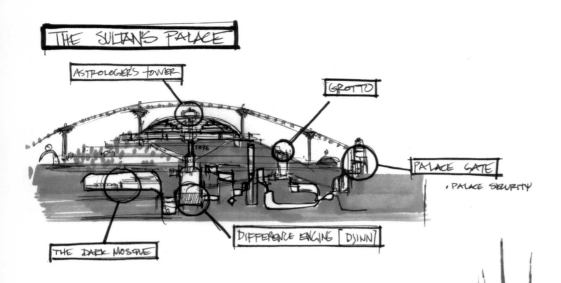

THE SULTAN'S PALACE

ASTROLOGER'S TOWER
GROTTO
PALACE GATE
PALACE SECURITY
THE DARK MOSQUE
DIFFERENCE ENGINE [DJINN]

THIEVES OF MARRAKECH

Thom: Set in the future in the bustling metropolis of Marrakech, *Thieves of Marrakech* is a visually *noir*, stealth-based game that features complicated environmental puzzles.

At the heart of Marrakech lies the Sultan's palace, a private compound that consists of a vast, tiered garden crowned with a luxurious palace entirely enclosed within a gigantic, engineered dome. The palace is an environmentally controlled paradise for the royal family that is walled off from the polluted city outside. The compound is built over the ruins of the ancient city, now a mysterious, haunted subterranean world below the palace gardens. The player is the leader of a band of thieves who have planned the ultimate heist: to rob the Sultan's palace.

I researched medieval Islamic art and architecture, especially the elaborately detailed, geometrically complex Moorish designs of the period. There is an incredibly rich palette of materials, shapes, forms and patterns to be found in traditional Islamic art and it was a challenge applying them to "future" architecture in a way that brought a sense of history to the designs but did not too literally borrow from the source. Orthographic sketches show a rough layout of the Sultan's complex and the locations of key spaces. Thumbnail sketches explore possible views of the lush garden level environments.

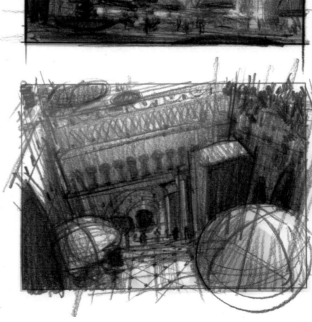

THOM TENERY

THIEVES OF MARRAKECH

Thom: The palace garden is designed as a series of complicated environmental puzzles. While it is heavily fortified and inaccessible from the outside, the extensive plumbing infrastructure required to irrigate the massive garden complex provides opportunities for clever thieves to gain access. The colossal machines necessary to pump water up from the canals, cycle it through the garden, and drain it are inherently weak points in the security. These sketches explore possible spaces encountered by thieves stealthing their way in to the palace garden.

An abandoned stone quarry *(upper left)* from which the ancient city itself was originally built has been left open for thieves daring enough to scale the slick stone faces. A labyrinth of engineered vegetation and a network of secret passages provide cover for the player's band of thieves. A sump and grated sewer duct *(right)* are ideal locations to pass into the garden undetected.

THIEVES OF MARRAKECH

Thom: The palace gate *(above left)* is intended to be an imposing but elegant portal in the fortress-like barrier wall that separates the destitute masses that inhabit the congested metropolis outside from royalty within. After arriving at a massing and scale that were appropriate, I explored different ways to articulate the opening with traditional Islamic motifs. A color sketch of the city outside of the palace complex *(above right)* shows a royal shuttle weaving through an urban canyon, two high-rise structures with cantilevered upper levels and a distinctive edge shape, a Moorish detail applied at the scale of a building. Concepts for the palace entry *(right)* show a heavily ornamented formal entrance court. The color painting on page 120 is an updated version of this idea, intended to achieve a more futuristic look.

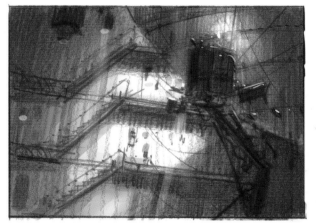

THIEVES OF MARRAKECH

Thom: The cruel Sultan that rules over the city is under supernatural control of the Djinn, an ancient, demonic creature that lives deep below the palace gardens in the ruins of the former palace. The centerpiece of the Djinn's lair is an enormous "difference engine," a machine that he uses to make predictions: information that is key to the Sultan's political power and stranglehold over the city. These sketches are exploring possible forms the difference engine might take, ranging from high-tech machines to a less complicated, stacked block configuration. Lighting is addressed at the initial sketch stage because it is such an important component of the space and story.

THIEVES OF MARRAKECH

Thom: The final objective is for the player to gain access to the heavily fortified Sultan's palace. In this scene, the thieves await the arrival of the prince and then make a bold attempt to walk through the front door. Powerful Djinn "magic" will prevent their entry as invisible guards materialize and attack. Intelligent landscape drones hovering nearby can merely observe the event, powerless to protect the royal family. Vehicles and architectural elements in this piece were inspired by medieval Islamic art objects including lanterns, incense burners, intricately carved Koranic stands, and elaborate stucco architectural details. Towering cypress trees recall the vegetation of the great Moorish palaces of Spain. Exaggerated color and lighting further enhance the drama of the scene. Light streams into the cavernous spaces below the palace through sewer gratings *(right)*, illuminating an ancient city wall and one of many crumbling ruins encountered on this level.

THOM TENERY

THIEVES OF MARRAKECH

Thom: Thieves encounter The Dark Mosque, which lies deep beneath the palace gardens in the sunless world of the Djinn. This treacherous subterranean world is inhabited by shape-shifting ghuls—malevolent spirits—the diseased, lunatics, and depraved rival thieves in search of valuable relics. Mysterious derelict structures and ancient artifacts provide clues to the nature of the old city and its buried secrets. It is discovered that, at great price to its population, the palace and its gardens were built over the old city, now a haunted catacomb. Thieves camp near a monumental patinaed gold dome *(left)* and prepare to infiltrate the palace from below.

THOM TENERY

121

Robh Ruppel:

Visual Development is first and foremost a design process. As such it addresses the challenge of using the fundamentals of art and design to come up with a new arrangement of shapes and colors that excite and inspire. Underneath every interesting piece of art is an excellent abstract design lurking behind the scenes. A piece of art succeeds or fails more on the principles of design than a glossy surface. It's these unheralded abstractions that give the art life. They are the plot twists and varying tempo of the visual art world. Without them, the drawing or painting lies flat, bleating out a monotonous tone neither engaging nor beckoning the viewer. It's because this foundation is so important that we push the design aspect over technique. There is a famous quote attributed to Stanley Kubrick. One of his last checks when filming goes, "Is there anything going on worth filming?" The same can be said for the design. Are there any ideas here that are interesting? Before you spend days rendering something, does it have a design?

The tools we work with are simple; shape: color, light and shadow. Good shapes are identifiable and simple—they are unique and easily remembered. A good design uses a few basic, varying shapes to complete the idea. Ian McCaig talks about the brilliance of Darth Vader's design. A skull in a Nazi helmet. Wow! If that doesn't conjure subconscious fear, then what does? Its effectiveness lies in its simplicity.

If the color of a design is pleasing in a simple, flat, abstract way, then by adding the modeling of light and shadow, it will stay well designed. But no amount of wrist work will save something where no pre-thought was put into it. If the light and shadow pattern make the object or scene easy to comprehend and enhance the form then they are successful in their explanation. A good designer can and should be able to make a scene interesting and readable in the fewest values. Look at the work of great painters and how they use the shape of the shadow to explain the form. It's never random, but simple and purposeful. Caravaggio's paintings are still powerful when reduced to merely two values; can the same be said of some art today? That is why design is so important and separates great art from art that is merely acceptable.

GATES OF HORN by Thom Tenery

DOROTHY

Victoria: These are designs for Dorothy from *The Wizard of Oz*. Sometimes when I'm not feeling particularly inspired, I do a few quick paintings to try and get an idea of what I want from the character. For this project, I first drew a number of silhouettes and then traced over them in pen to get an interesting design within the silhouette. Eventually I settled on a ballerina-esque design. On this page is a set of color samples I did for the costume. I tried out many different styles to get different feelings for the character, varying from spunky to dark to light and insubstantial.

DOROTHY

Victoria: To me, Dorothy always felt like a character who was passive in the story, where most of the things are happening *to* her and one of the few active things she does is by accident. On this page is a rendering of the final design chosen from the color samples. I wanted her to feel innocent and doll-like to make her seem more passive. I put her in a traditional ballerina pose and kept as much of the spirit that the original drawing had in it as possible.

WATER VS. FIRE
CITYSCAPE AT DUSK

Sho: The characters here were developed for a story that takes place in a world where two tribes are fighting with each other. The left two characters belong to the Water Tribe, which is sophisticated and has a larger population. The far right character belongs to the Fire Tribe, which is more primitive and has a small village-unit. Since the setup was that they use magic and are traveling, I determined that heavy armored costumes were going to look ridiculous. *(continued on opposite page)*

After researching various cultures in different ages and regions, I found that two ancient Japanese cultures, Jomon and Yayoi, represent each social structure and the characters of water and fire. Extracting form languages from the products of their cultures, I applied them to these character designs.

Simon: *(opposite page, bottom)* This version of a huge sci-fi cityscape pushed my skills to a new level in terms of indicating massive amounts of detail in the most efficient manner possible. In the end the lesson was this: more detail requires more time. I had no idea. The piece was painted over many times, but the idea remained the same. This city is one dirty place.

PALACE GARDEN

Marcus: For this palace garden I first began with several, rough line drawings at the left, before coming to a final decision. The illustration above has my desired feeling of foreground, middle ground and background as well as a feeling of scale. I scanned the drawing into Photoshop and put in the value. It is useful to use the artistic filter cutout in Photoshop to get a clear "read" of the shadow shapes and the areas of most contrast. I can then go back to the original drawing in Photoshop and make adjustments accordingly before painting in color.

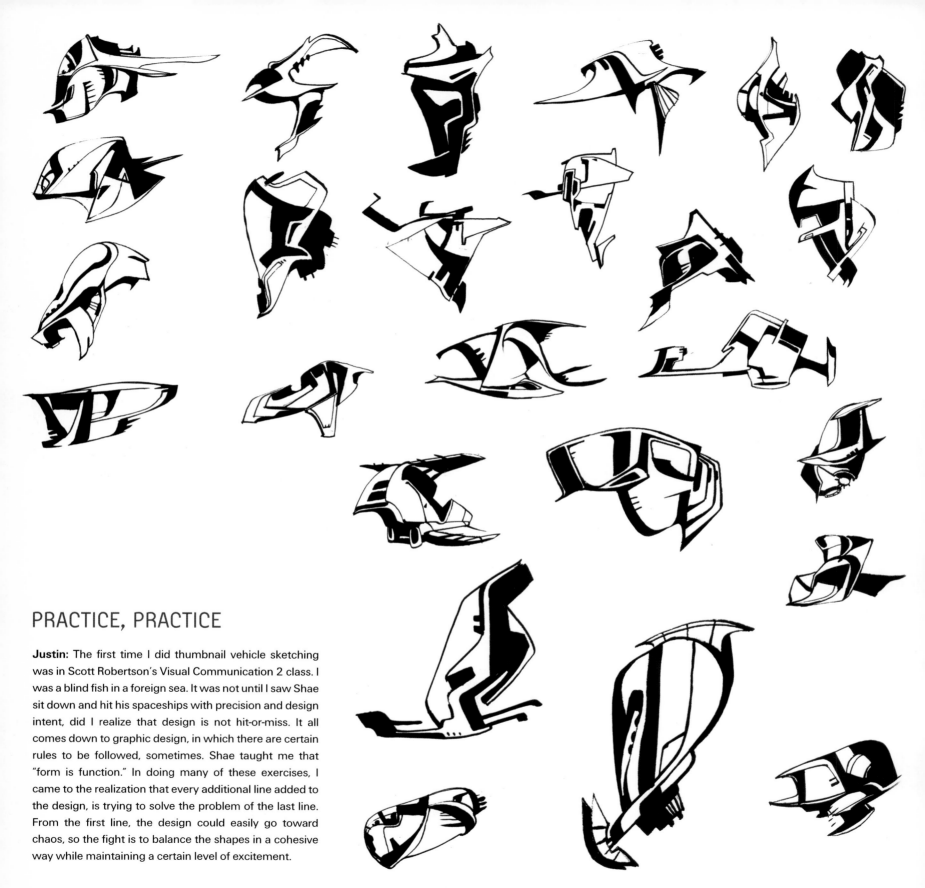

PRACTICE, PRACTICE

Justin: The first time I did thumbnail vehicle sketching was in Scott Robertson's Visual Communication 2 class. I was a blind fish in a foreign sea. It was not until I saw Shae sit down and hit his spaceships with precision and design intent, did I realize that design is not hit-or-miss. It all comes down to graphic design, in which there are certain rules to be followed, sometimes. Shae taught me that "form is function." In doing many of these exercises, I came to the realization that every additional line added to the design, is trying to solve the problem of the last line. From the first line, the design could easily go toward chaos, so the fight is to balance the shapes in a cohesive way while maintaining a certain level of excitement.

JUSTIN PICHETRUNGSI

JUSTIN PICHETRUNGSI

129

A DUSTY INDUSTRIAL DAY

Justin: As I just mentioned about the process of problem solving for vehicle design, I honestly believe that the same principles apply to a composition in shot design. Except now the actual, rectangular frame is an important element in balancing the shapes and masses. Interesting design is established by the level of compositional "dynamism." Equal proportion and equal massing will create a static and boring design. Pushing for dynamic proportion, designing positive and negative shapes, along with creating a visual path are some tools for achieving interesting composition.

JUSTIN PICHETRUNGSI

JUSTIN PICHETRUNGSI

SCI-FI CITYSCAPE

Shae: After reading the synopsis I was left with the impression that the environment we were asked to design would be claustrophobic, uncomfortable and run-down by over-use. With these feelings in mind I was searching for solutions with lots of visual traffic, pollution, and details that expressed deterioration. I like to generate many ideas so I started by doing many small black and white sketches. I also enjoy switching things up with my media so I began some grayscale marker sketches seen to the right.

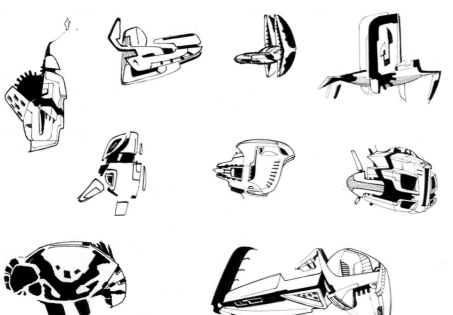
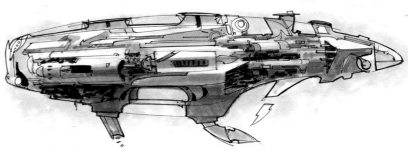

SCI-FI CITYSCAPE & SHIPS

Shae: The sketches above are some refined variations of my urban environment. Up to this point I was trying to figure out what the main statement of the place was going to be. Once that was accomplished through the sketching process on the facing page, it was time to fine-tune what the space was going to convey to its viewers through many trials of the same basic foundation.

Another passion of mine is the drawing of vehicles. These were for a ship that is as huge as it is fast. I wanted to convey the energy of the ship and create some provocative shapes.

Scott Robertson:

In the desire to create something truly original for the entertainment world a designer is faced first, with a blank piece of paper and second, with a client asking him or her to design, draw and render something the world has never seen before. This, as you can imagine, is a daunting task. It was with this in mind that I asked fellow designer Nick Pugh, renowned for his abilities to create unique forms and apply them to a variety of subject matter, to help bring this class into being.

This course focuses on some of his techniques used to create a unique form language that can then be applied to the design of environments, characters, vehicles and props. Students are trained to utilize a range of research methods to better understand story and timeframes appropriate to the narrative. In addition, they practice a variety of quick sketching techniques to help realize and discover their unique forms. At the end of the course they build a 3-D model, which exemplifies their new design language created throughout the term, utilizing the creative philosophies introduced by Nick.

As a designer and educator, this class has become one of my favorites to observe throughout each term. The creative aesthetic paths the students find themselves exploring provide a very fresh departure from the production-oriented, real-world design jobs I am so often exposed to. As this course matures and builds an even stronger place in the fourth-term line-up of classes, I look into the future with great expectations of further visual delight.

ROBOT by Peter Chan

SEARCHING FOR ORIGINALITY

Craig: Originality is a magical and mysterious animal that pokes her head out at odd times during my creative process. Sometimes her presence is obvious, and other times she remains unseen. While studying with the valiant Nick Pugh, I had an opportunity to seek out this beast and employ her to help me create a personal form language. With my pencil and paper in hand I set out on a journey to do just that. I searched high and low through nonsensical sleep-deprived scribbles, and musically inspired sketchy clumps of graphite. It seemed the more drawing I did, the farther I took myself from finding originality! I realized that I was falling into moving through old muscle habits of sketching and my subconscious was enforcing these mundane forms. So I turned back and began again, this time reinventing my process. I found inspiration in science journals and pop-culture trends and managed to represent it photographically. I cut out and glued together fragments of the world around me then used that as a new point of departure. I even held my pencil in ways that even the nimblest of men would find challenging! Hundreds of pieces of paper later I found myself at the end of an arduous journey only to realize that Originality can't always be summoned at my whim. She is much more process-dependant and becomes more visible each time I embark on a creative journey in a new and fresh way. Often times, the destination becomes just as magical and original as the path that brought me there. Here are a few of the unique creatures I came across while searching for Originality.

CRAIG SHOJI

M RMOR

Gino: I had a lot of fun playing with the idea of a substance that could be manipulated from a liquid state into a solid, for a defensive purpose such as armor. I was inspired by a liquid called MR fluid, which can turn from liquid to solid when an electrical current is applied. I imagined the liquid swirling and shifting around the soldier, solidifying to protect vital areas or regions under attack. It was later in my research that I learned that technology close to this is actually being researched today.

 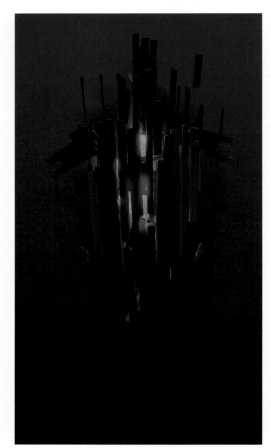 

TRANS-DIMENSIONAL EXISTENCE

Eric: The inspiration for these pieces came from an idea I had about how a two-dimensional object might look if forced to exist in three dimensions. The first piece of the series was the character at the top of the page. The images were created by making random marks on folded pieces of paper, then unfolding the paper and layering the marks. The form was created from the result by over-painting the shapes in Photoshop. I moved the concept into 3-D using Alias Studio for the craft shown to the right. Instead of randomly placed marks, I played with the Alias surfacing tools to push and pull planes and splines. The subsequent forms and wire-frames were taken into Photoshop and manipulated for the result seen here.

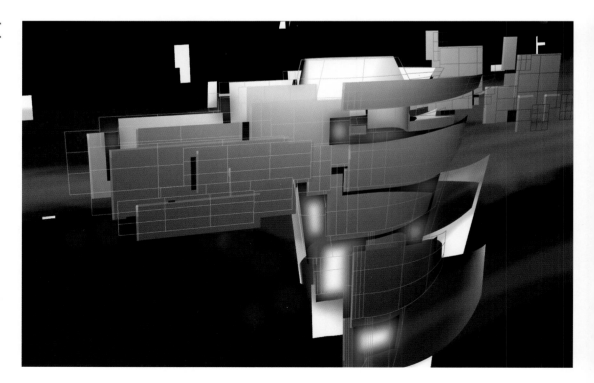

ERIC LUTES

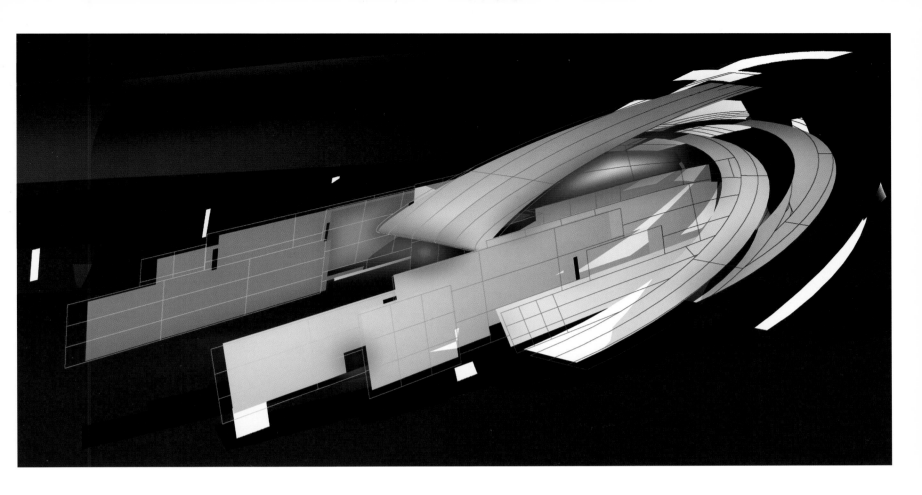

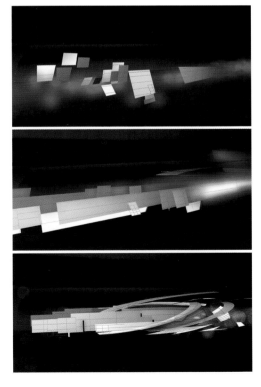

IMPRACTICAL CRAFT

Eric: If something was forced to cross dimensions, then all conventional rules could be abandoned, even traditional methods of locomotion. The craft on this page are meant to look as though they are barely keeping cohesion. Only the thin wire matrix around them keeps the individual parts from escaping each other. These were a lot of fun to do because they allowed me to throw symmetry out the window and focus more on abstract aesthetics.

For traveling, I thought that the two-dimensional parts would have to separate before being able to cross over. Once inside a three-dimensional world, it could reassemble and continue on its journey.

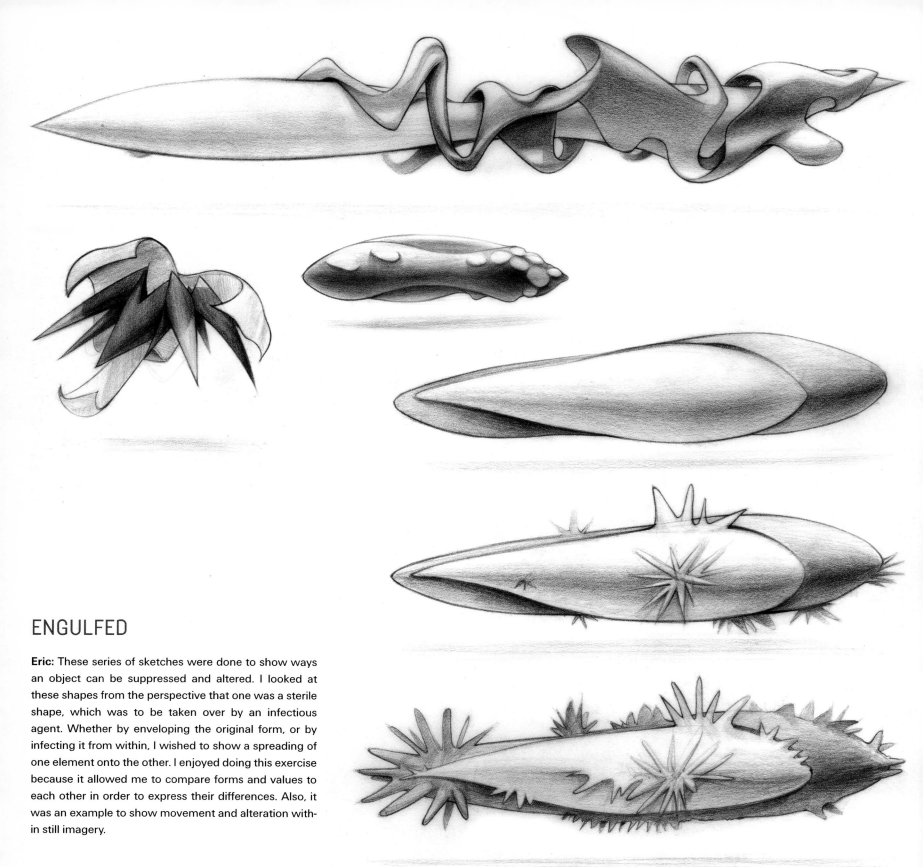

ENGULFED

Eric: These series of sketches were done to show ways an object can be suppressed and altered. I looked at these shapes from the perspective that one was a sterile shape, which was to be taken over by an infectious agent. Whether by enveloping the original form, or by infecting it from within, I wished to show a spreading of one element onto the other. I enjoyed doing this exercise because it allowed me to compare forms and values to each other in order to express their differences. Also, it was an example to show movement and alteration within still imagery.

ERIC NG

BIOLUMINESCENCE

Eric: Utilizing droplets of colored ink in water as inspiration, I created an underwater city. I thought it would be interesting to create a structure originating from a form language that was organic and free flowing. The food coloring was able to produce a rich color yet at the same time create layers of transparencies. I wished to show the structure built around a core of light in suspension throughout a liquid. The city itself was to be powered with bioluminescence much like that of deep-sea marine life. As it flows through the city, it creates a cloud of energy that illuminates its surroundings.

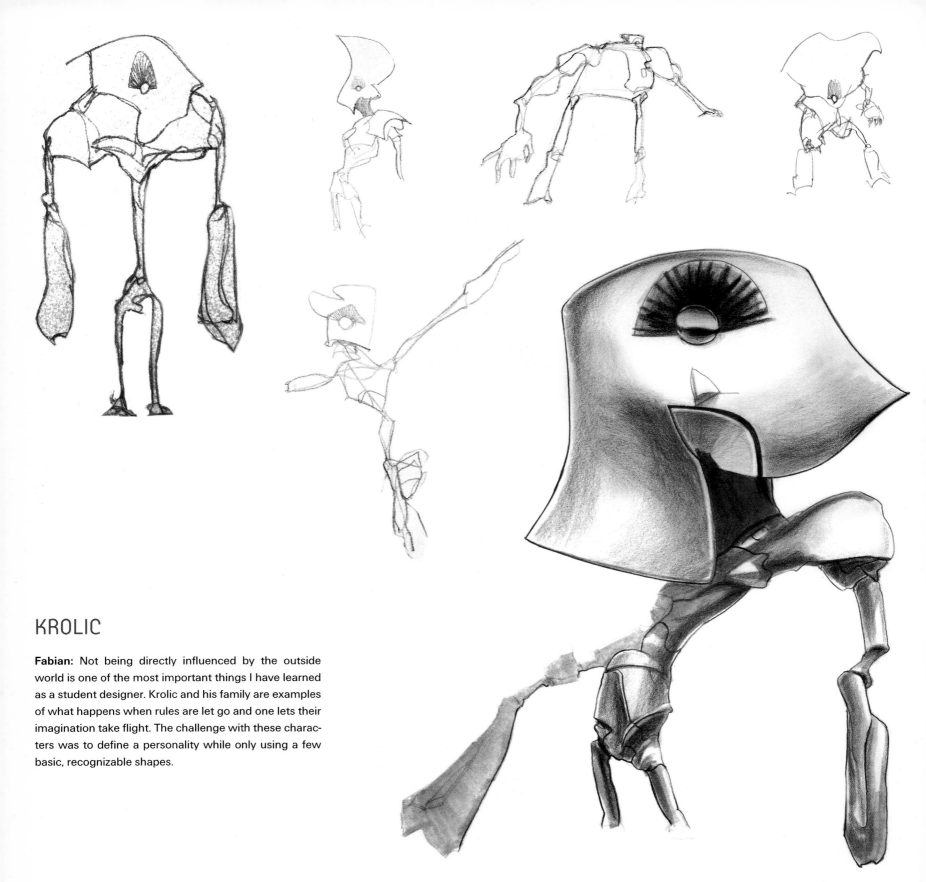

KROLIC

Fabian: Not being directly influenced by the outside world is one of the most important things I have learned as a student designer. Krolic and his family are examples of what happens when rules are let go and one lets their imagination take flight. The challenge with these characters was to define a personality while only using a few basic, recognizable shapes.

FABIAN LACEY

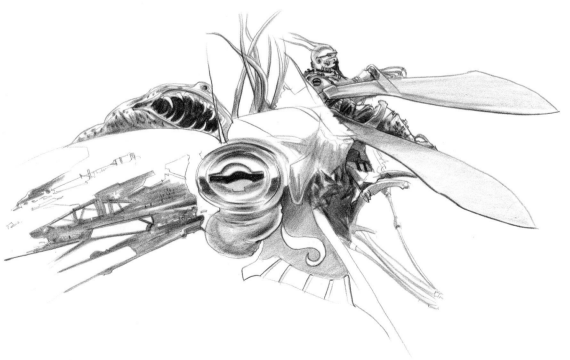

NOISY SKIES

Fabian: Dwelling below the carbon-filled fumes, people can hear the high-pitched screams emitted by the Hydlix engines. In Vagab, vehicles roam the skies as they travel through thick layers of smoke-infused gas. It doesn't take much to negotiate maneuvers with the authoritative beast once it's pointed in the right direction. However, there are few who truly understand how to harness its ability to dance among the clouds.

FABIAN LACEY

DISTANCE

Marcus: A boy is lost in a future video game world. The game utilizes memories to create a unique, personal video-game experience. To create the concepts for this project I simply sat down at my desk and let my pen move across the page without giving it too much thought. My goal was to create something common-place that one had never seen before. Without looking at reference or inspiration, the only things you are working with are memories and creativity. This story is about just that. The main character is trapped in a world that is con-structed and operated by memories and personal creativ-ity. The result is an abstract universe based on everyday visual stimuli.

MARCUS COLLINS

MATTER

Marcus: Items such as telephone wires, shingles from old rooftops, fences, the traffic lights that hang over the streets as we make our daily commute to work and other things we barely think about but are a part of our visual lives, are incorporated in the environments that I have created. The black matter in these pieces represents the abstract patterns and forms that are undefined by our mind but help create the unique world. The matter is structured and very tight in some areas, while in others it is uncontrolled and organic, representing architecture and nature. I used ink in two different ways to create these effects. For the tighter strokes I used a wide marker and for the looser effect I blew ink across the page creating an uncontrolled pattern.

MARCUS COLLINS

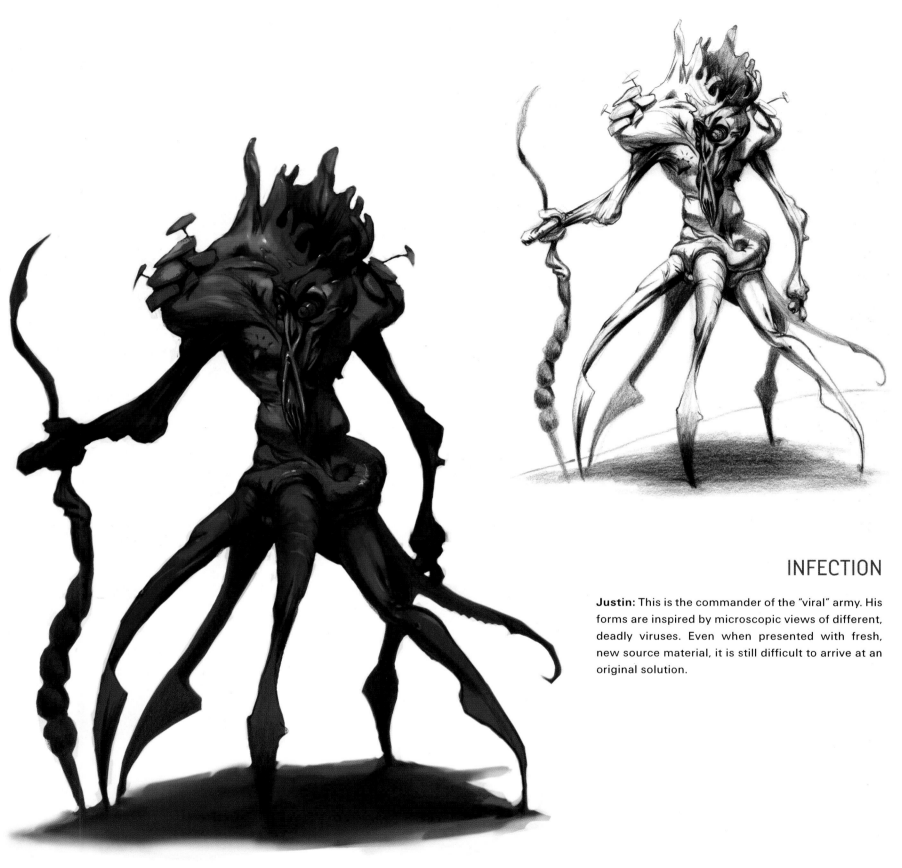

INFECTION

Justin: This is the commander of the "viral" army. His forms are inspired by microscopic views of different, deadly viruses. Even when presented with fresh, new source material, it is still difficult to arrive at an original solution.

JUSTIN PICHETRUNGSI

SAMPLING

Justin: During the second half of our term, I developed a story based on the AIDS virus and cancer. The bad guys' forms are inspired by compiling molecular diagrams of the AIDS virus and cancerous cells. The good guys are inspired by the diagrams of the cures for such viruses. This technique is called "sampling." Top left, you can still see the source material. This character is the "Hermes" of our story, carrying a crossbow. Elements of his costume contain the helixes of DNA and the phospholipid structure of the cell membrane.

JUSTIN PICHETRUNGSI

LEADING LADIES

Justin: Nick Pugh was very adamant about using the source material directly. He pulled a piece of tracing paper and started drawing over my graphs and diagrams, directly copying and eliminating elements he liked or disliked, which is the technique behind the piece on the right. In the left piece, I wanted to throw a "viral" twist onto a circus-inspired costume. The middle piece is all about using the "cure" ribbons as the main form language. A big struggle with using an "originality" technique is that it takes a lot of restraint on the part of the designer. Entropy and chaos is the nature of the beast. In searching for new and exciting forms, the start will be messy and complicated, and it is up to the designer to harness a newly invented original form language, if possible.

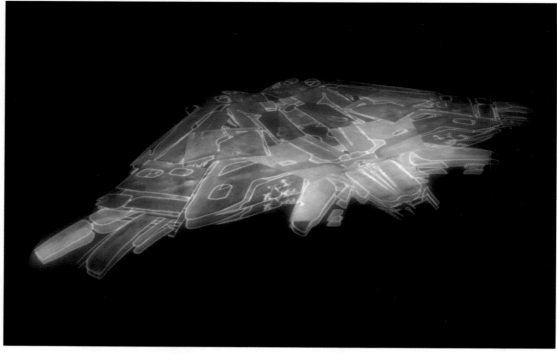

NANO WORLD

David: For Originality in Design, our instructor, Nick Pugh, helped us devise unique ways of coming up with original form languages. The technique I developed started with random scribbles within the Corel Painter program; generally horizontal for vehicles, vertical for characters and to the edges of a composition for environments. I would then take a sample of a graphic texture, in this case crystals under an electron microscope, cut it up into arbitrary collage pieces, then use the scribble component as a structural guide. Above are two examples of early modeling solutions utilizing geometry with the collage graphic projected on it within the 3-D modeling program, Maya. These vehicles seemed otherworldly and celestial to me—I envisioned the craft being made up of microscopic nano-components surrounded by a clear membrane able to accommodate the movements of the underlying segments in order to facilitate mobility.

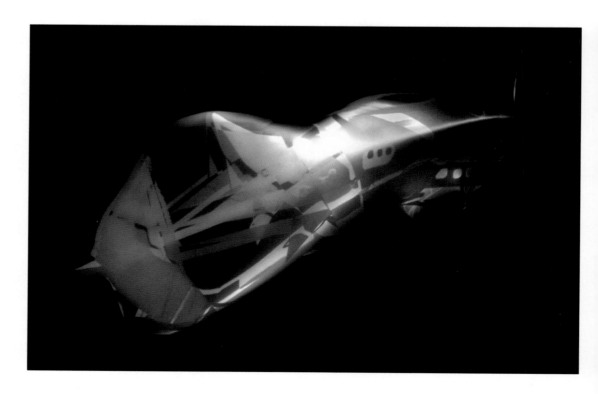

DAVID HOBBINS

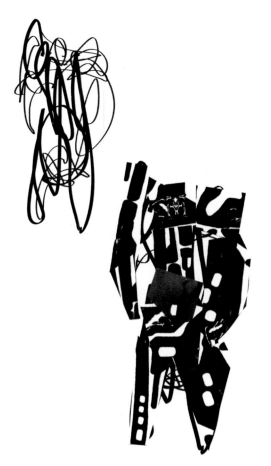

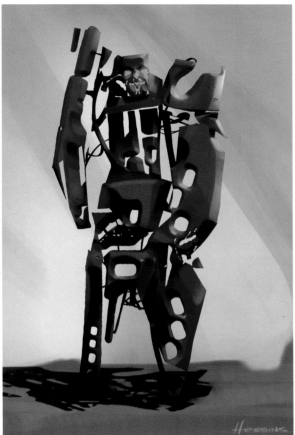

NANO WORLD

David: Nano World is the story of a young boy in the near future who is suffering from a brain tumor. As a last resort to save the boy's life, the doctors attempt a risky procedure that involves the use of intelligent nanotechnology. The race of nanobots destroys the tumor, but then something unexpected happens. A violent mutiny occurs among the nanobots and the host boy is held hostage in a dangerous coma. But there are nanobots who have escaped being reprogrammed and they rally against the rogue group. Seeking an ally, the resistance chooses the boy. Because of their brain expertise, liberating nanobots tap into the boy's unconscious mind and enlist his body's natural microscopic fighters. All the while, the boy believes his inner-space adventure is only a wild dream. On this page, I have an example of a Nano World character and an inner- space environment inspired by this originality technique. The 3-D model above is carved out of 10-pound foam and served as a form test for my final project.

DAVID HOBBINS

FLASH MOB FIRE TANK

Simon: These forms were inspired by the social phenomenon known as flash mobbing. Flash mobbing consists of random individuals who meet at a designated place to perform a certain action together. I simplified this concept into using smaller units orbiting around and becoming a larger being, while still maintaining their own individuality. Though each piece looks similar, they are in fact, unique. Translating this into characters and vehicles was a challenge as a balance had to be found between the individual particles and the whole.

SIMON KO

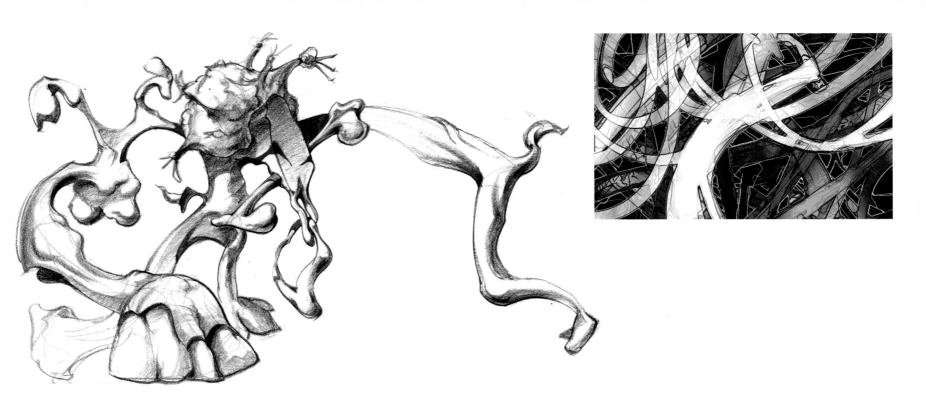

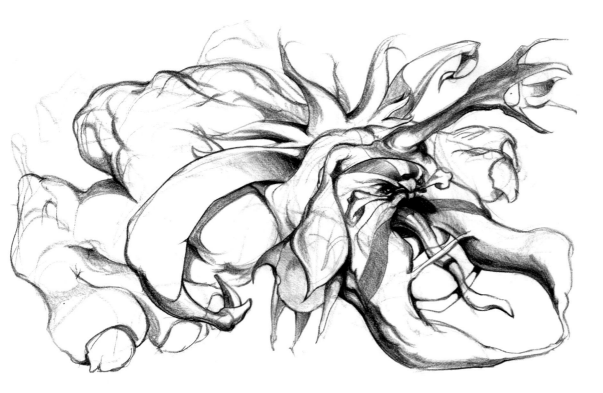

KRUMP

Hamzah: Finding inspiration in a new social movement was an interesting approach to design. I immediately thought about the evolution of the hip-hop culture and how krumping was recently brought into the mainstream in Los Angeles. In terms of graphics, a lot of influence still carried on from the 80s "Wild-Style" graffiti into modern krump graphics. In the dancing, there are lots of rapid hand gestures, upper body movements, low stances, grounded footwork, and body language that had to run with the music. With that in mind, I tried to sketch what I felt krumping would look like in an overall graphic and form language. The results on this page are pretty intense and were an eye-opener for me. Finding some video of krumping online is worth the research.

THE DESIGN

Darren: This concept is of a futuristic megalopolis structure, constructed of a single unit comprised of several sub-dominant architectural components.

My process behind this project was based on two 18 x 24-inch mixed media traditional paintings applied over stretched canvas, which were completed at the inception of the project. The objective was to use the two original pieces of art as the style guides for the entire production design of my venture. The paintings were based on a technique using a grid-masking pattern. Dripping acrylic paint (Ink, Heptane, Xylene, methyl ethyl ketone, enamel) multiple times in different directions. Then repeating the process in layers to create a completely original outcome that was similar yet varied in each separate piece. Upon completion, I scanned the works and digitally composited sections on multiple adjustment layers in Photoshop. I was looking for interesting compositions and design silhouettes that I could use later to create these environments, architecture and vehicles.

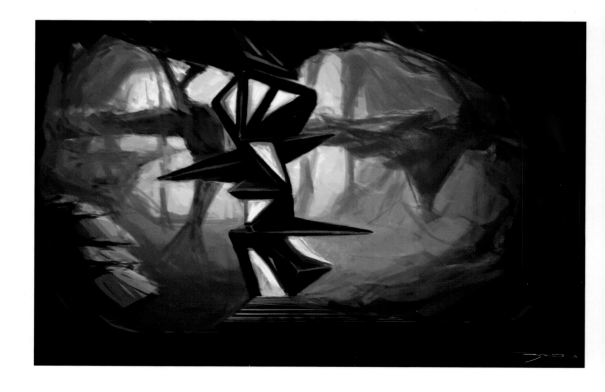

AIR SHIP

Darren: The design for this aircraft was also found using the digital compositing techniques I previously outlined. Incorporating several multiplied, opacity-jittered layers of my original, mixed-media paintings, I found interesting silhouettes of a localized drip pattern section and immediately began rendering and exploring form found in the randomized patterns. After completing the first digital painting you see above, "Ship Arriving," I moved directly to mocking up a foam core model in 3-D, and drafting plans for the final scale model you see to the left. This model was constructed using traditional model-making techniques. The main forms were carved from laminated medium density fiberboard; other materials include aluminum, and styrene.

DARREN BACON

IN SEARCH OF ELYSIUM

Kevin: My goal with the above images was to experiment with process to create a unique form language. I combined several different image-making methodologies: scanning objects and photos, collaging them together, painting, and manipulating everything in Photoshop to eventually come up with forms that I thought were interesting. I then used these forms as inspiration for designing environments and creatures. As I designed, I imagined a lost soul searching his way through purgatory or another uncomfortable place in the afterlife, where the laws of physics are distorted, with creatures and landscapes adhering to the distorted rules to create a realm that is truly bizarre.

KEVIN SWARTZ

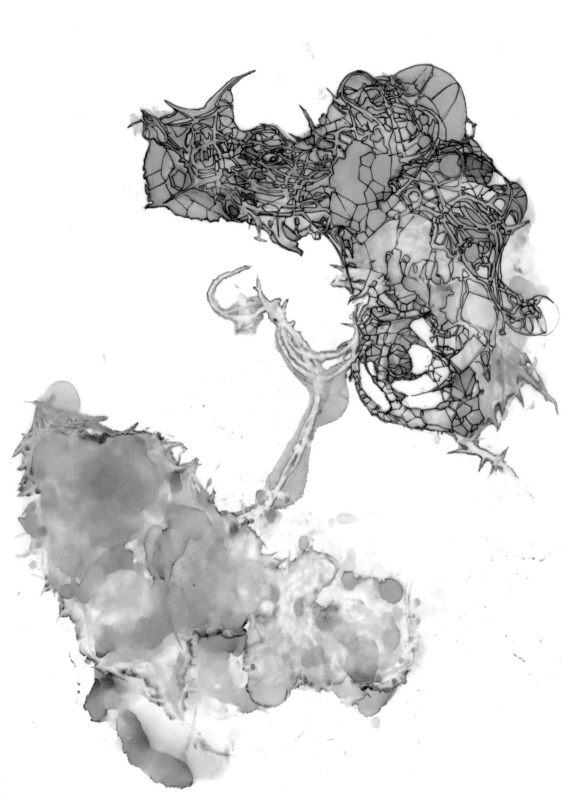

UNTITLED

Raj: The work above was inspired by the cultural revolution of connectivity that our scientific and technological progress has achieved. Instantaneous communication, sharing of information through the World Wide Web, and even relatively recent theories in physics (such as string theory) express an ever-increasing connectivity between all things.

The work is a result of masses of hair (thanks Bets!) on vellum with gray ink applied to the surface. The ink was allowed to slowly intercalate along the surface, following the intricate paths each strand of hair had created. The resulting abstractions then became the structure upon which I drew, using either pencil or pen. The ink-hair structure was strictly adhered to and the form, proportions and aesthetic were derived by this process of "connectivity."

FEVER DREAM

Raj: The character and creature designs here are the result of a process derived from a dream sequence. Nick asked us to use an intense, emotional experience or a dream to develop a process resulting in a unique form language. Since I was young, I have had a recurring nightmare in which my comforter actually engulfs and slowly devours me (strange, I know). The feelings from this dream are so visceral I can readily recall the horror, desperation and fear days later. To capture these nightmarish experiences, I actually took digital photos of my comforter and drew and painted over them. I feel the results really embody the creepiness and fear involved in my nightmare.

The environments on this page are a result of the process derived from connectivity discussed earlier. Referred to as my "hair drawings" by my classmates, I found this process to be incredibly exploratory and exciting. Unlike the drawings for architecture, these environments allowed me to explore atmosphere and organic form over tangi-

ble and recognizable structure. The piece at the top is a long shot of the environment showing its scale and depth, without expressing its specific location. Is it underground? Floating in space? I wanted to create this sense of ambiguity and yet still have a sense of depth and intricacy to the world.

The two images at the bottom are the most tangible ideas of structures within the confines of the evolving world. I wanted to create unique pieces of architecture that fit into this strange form language that was developing. The technique never allowed me to use traditional perspective drawing techniques; any sense of depth to the world is due to the use of limited space, by simply overlapping various structures. I wanted the buildings to have the same haphazard and organic development as my past work, but still have a sense of place and solidity.

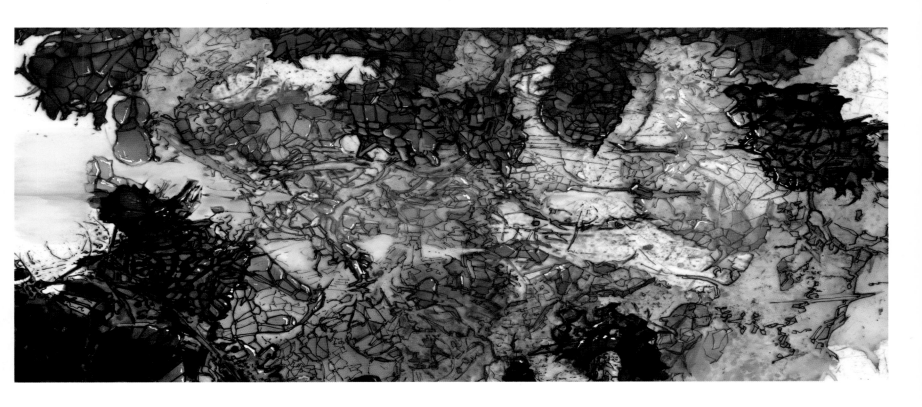

RAJ RIHAL

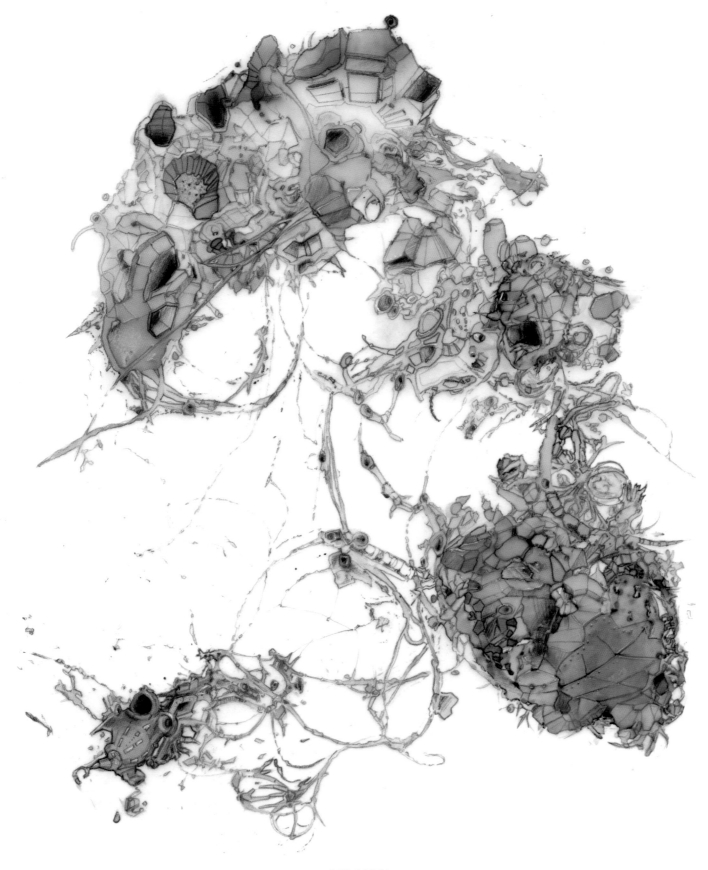

RAJ RIHAL

JALOPY

Raj: *(left)* This final piece is a vehicle existing in the world depicted on the previous pages. The process in development was the same, but in this instance I wanted to create a "space jalopy" traveling the universe. With a variety of misaligned parts, it is barely holding together and yet manages to travel great distances. To me, the sinuous attachments between parts, and the larger area floating above the tiny "cockpit" at the very bottom, elicits a feeling of a vehicle/structure able to float or travel through a vacuum.

PHOTON SHIELD

Peter: *(above)* This was the final piece for my originality project. I had been using only one brush in Photoshop for all the paintings I did, and I thought it was perfect for the shield effect and texture. My main idea was to have floating wrist-armor for the character that could be transformed into different gear. In this scene, the wrist armor quickly spools out a photon-textile that is woven into a spherical shield.

NATURAL BRUSH #12

Peter: There are so many great tools to create images within Photoshop that it sometimes gives me a headache. For the Originality class, I experimented with different painting techniques and narrowed my tools down to using just one brush for all the work.

With the natural brush #12, I found that I could get the painterly quality that I love in oil paintings, as well as a variety of dynamic movement within the texture and color. Using only one tool speeds up my creative process tremendously.

PETER CHAN

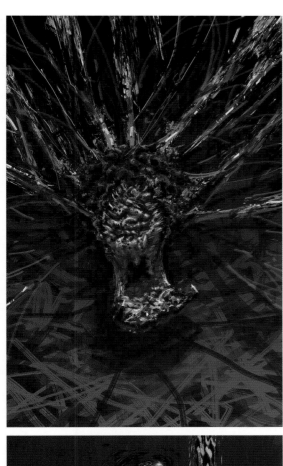

NATURAL BRUSH STUDIES

Peter: Here are some examples of character design that were done with the same brush and process.

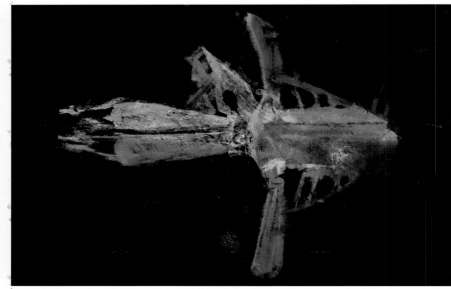

UNDERSEA VEHICLES

Sho: The three vehicle designs on this page were developed with the purpose of achieving original and unique designs. Besides these three, I did about twenty designs including environments and creatures. The process that I took was designing from the unexpected shapes that I could get by the layering of bones. After multiplying approximately fifty layers of photos of animal skeletons in Photoshop, I experimented with switching on/off each layer, changing each blending mode, changing the order, and zooming in on the various micro compositions. The aim was keeping the beautiful shapes of bones in a micro view and making a different entity like a vehicle or an environment in a macro view.

SHO KATAYAMA

BUILDERING

Thom: The solo sport of urban climbing, also known as buildering, is one of the more radical activities to appear on the extreme sports scene in recent years. Buildering has its roots in the sport of rock climbing, but involves the more dangerous technique of free-climbing large, urban structures without the use of climbing equipment. A subversive form of expression, akin to graffiti, it is a kind of urban performance art for those daring enough to undertake it. My goal was to extract a visual language from the activity and then transform it into a form language that could be applied to a range of objects and environments. Just as the more traditional sport of rock climbing involves dozens of common physical positions and techniques, urban climbers can be seen in a number of dynamic poses appropriate to the wide variety of obstacles they encounter in the urban terrain. These sketches represent visual abstractions of these positions. Using dozens of photos of urban climbers in action as reference, I abstracted these positions as "character shapes" with a brush pen. These character shapes became the graphic basis of the constructs shown here. Using pen, marker, and black chalk for value gradations, I have built a library of forms that can be applied to a range of objects and environments. The result retains something of the aggressive and dynamic character of the sport without being too literal of an interpretation. This process of independently arriving at a form language that serves as the set of "form rules" for a designed world is useful because it yields unique shapes that would not otherwise have been discovered using straightforward drawing techniques. Do try this at home.

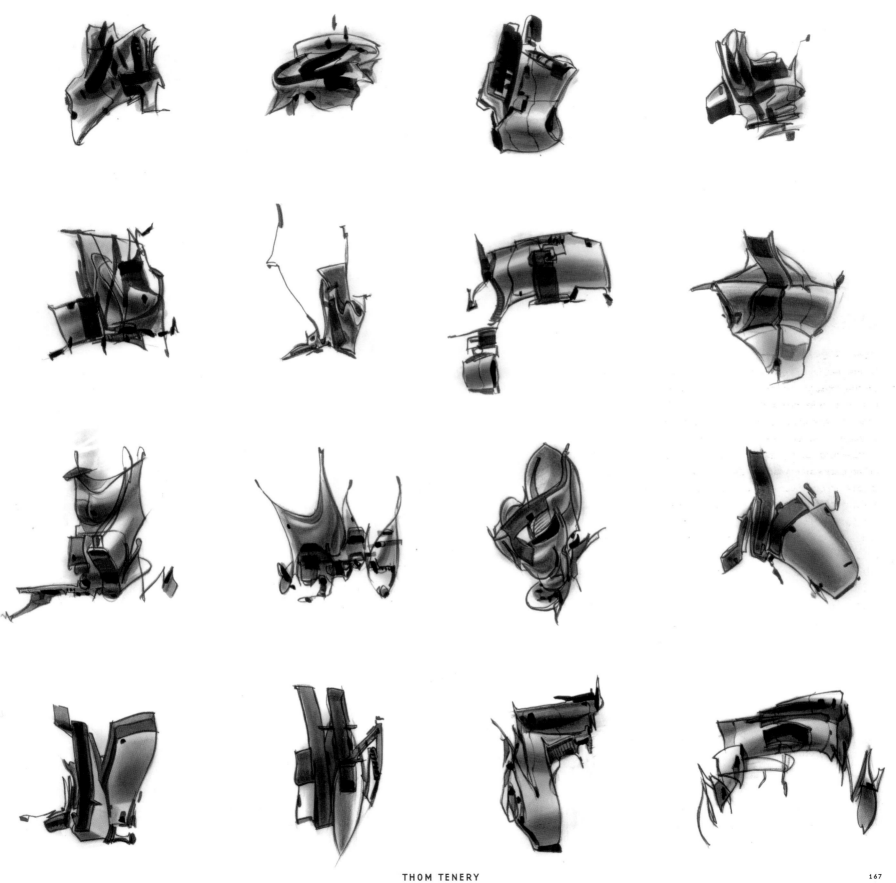

THOM TENERY

BUILDERING

Thom: The story that I was designing toward required a bold aesthetic in which environments and vehicles needed to have seamlessly blended organic and mechanical characteristics. They needed to look potentially dangerous without resorting to clichés. The environments and vehicles on page 165, and those seen here, are the result of digitally kitbashing several of the thumbnail sketches from the previous page. The scanned sketches were brought into Photoshop on separate layers and then manipulated with transform tools and arbitrarily combined via layer modes in order to arrive at interesting new shapes, graphics and proportions. This sampling technique adds an additional generation of transformation to the process, encourages happy accidents, and is a good way to generate unique imagery in a limited amount of time. The form language and essential character of the source material is retained in this process. It is then a matter of identifying the imagery with the most potential and applying materials and lighting to make it spatially real.

THOM TENERY

students

JONATHAN BACH

Jonathan Bach was born in Austin, Texas in 1981. He later moved to Southern California where he grew up with an interest in entrepreneurial endeavors and art. He drew as much as possible until he decided to invest in himself and take an Art Center night class at Mazda in Irvine. Jonathan later enrolled at Art Center as a transportation design major where he realized that entertainment design was a perfect fit for his eclectic interests. Jonathan now works at Spark Unlimited as a visual development artist and goes to Art Center College of Design. He plans to take a break to paint and explore the world before finishing his education.

Web site: www.Jbachdesign.com   E-mail: Turbineguy9@yahoo.com

DARREN BACON

Darren grew up in a small town in Washington state, raised by a family of industrial designers and engineers. He spent the majority of his free time drawing and designing. He obtained an Associate of Arts degree in Industrial Design Technology (2003) from the Art Institute of Seattle. While there, he was a member of a Honda-sponsored design project, and was encouraged to visit the Southern California Honda campus. During this Los Angeles tour, he was urged by Honda's designers to attend Art Center College of Design. Within a few weeks, Darren enrolled. He plans to graduate in 2007. Darren credits many of his instructors, mentors and family for their invaluable guidance, inspiration and support along the way.

Web site: www.darrenbacon.com   E-mail: darren@darrenbacon.com

PETER CHAN

Peter Chan was born in Taiwan and moved to Hong Kong at the age of 10. Interested in drawing and painting, Peter attended Interlochen Arts Academy in Michigan, U.S.A. where he began to focus his skills in fine arts. Afterwards, Peter received his B.F.A. at the Rhode Island School of Design where he changed majors: first from jewelry design to illustration and then to furniture design. In 2004, Peter moved to California and is currently attending Art Center College of Design for a Master's degree in industrial design. Peter is now focusing his studies in the Entertainment Design curriculum where he is certain he has finally found his home.

Web site: www.drawpeterdraw.com   E-mail: drawpeter@hotmail.com

MARCUS COLLINS

Marcus was born in Miami, Florida in 1985, and spent his childhood developing a strong interest in the visual arts. He attended Design and Architecture Senior High, and chose industrial design as a major. This program pushed the fundamentals of perspective and encouraged strong drawing technique. During the summer of his junior year, he was chosen among three other students in class to attend a two-week workshop at Art Center College of Design in Pasadena, California. After the trip he was inspired by the nature of excellence the college exuded and decided to attend. Marcus is now a full-time student at Art Center and is enjoying his third year. He is majoring in product design with a focus in entertainment design.

Web site: www.marcusacollins.com   E-mail: marcus@marcusacollins.com

DAVID HOBBINS

David Hobbins was born and raised in Vancouver, Canada. Originally trained as a 3-D animator, Hobbins did a quick stint at Mainframe Entertainment, later gaining fulltime employment as part of Electronic Arts' motion capture department, working on a wide range of titles from *Madden* to *The Lord of the Rings*. Inspired by the concept art on the studio walls, David quickly put together a portfolio, applied to Art Center College of Design and was accepted to the fall semester of 2004. David is currently working toward a B.S. in Transportation Design with a minor in Entertainment Design.

Web site: www.davidhobbins.com   E-mail: hobbins@artcenter.edu

HAMZAH KASOM

Hamzah was raised in Santa Ana, California (the O.C.), where he spent most of his childhood drawing. Struggling to major in something meaningful in college, he was introduced to commercial art by friends in the industry and then persuaded to try Art Center College of Design in the product design program. Taking advantage of the freedom of blue sky designs in school, Hamzah let his imagination take off while trying to constantly absorb new information, history and techniques about the world of art and design. Since then, Hamzah has had the opportunity to refine his skills and have experiences in a variety of industries, including games, web design, graphics, and animation. He plans to graduate in 2007, then travel the world.

Web site: www.hamzaHKasom.com   E-mail: ithamzah@yahoo.com

SHO KATAYAMA

Sho grew up in Tokyo, Japan. After working in the TV commercial industry for a couple of years, he moved to Los Angeles to attend Art Center. Although he started as a film major, he began drawing figures at workshops under the guidance of the illustration department, and soon transferred to that major. Inspired by Richard Schmid, Sho immersed himself in oil-painting techniques. Being fortunate to have splendid teachers like Michael Hussar, Michael Hernandez, and Kinman Chan, painting has constantly fascinated him. While continuing to paint from life, Sho spends most of his time on entertainment work. Applying his traditional skill to the entertainment industry, his goal is to become a core member of the creative group producing insightful, visual stories that remain in audiences' memories.
Web site: www.shokatayama.com   E-mail: katayama@artcenter.edu

SIMON KO

Originally from the San Francisco Bay area, Simon Ko came to Southern California to study at UC Irvine and eventually at Art Center College of Design. He began his entertainment career after studying five terms of Transportation Design. As an automotive enthusiast, he found it difficult to leave the Transportation Design curriculum, but eventually realized that the corporate world didn't suit his desired lifestyle. He believes that to improve oneself as a concept designer, one should see as much of the world as possible, experience different cultures, and meet new people. When not drawing, he enjoys photography, motorcycles, hiking, and playing the guitar. He has recently completed a 7-month internship with Spark Unlimited and is excited to complete his education to venture into the working world.
E-mail: simonko@gmail.com

FABIAN LACEY

Fabian Lacey is a Los Angeles-based concept designer, and has done work for Mattel, Coca-Cola, and Sony Entertainment. With emphasis on Entertainment Design, he is making his way through Art Center's Transportation Design program. Fabian is beginning his professional career by designing characters, creatures, vehicles and environments. He has spent much of his time at Art Center as a student teacher in Industrial Design for the Institute of Educational Advancement, and Mexico's Monterey Technologic University exchange program. Fabian plans to graduate in 2008 after a design internship with BMW Advanced Concepts Center in Munich, Germany in the summer of 2007.

Web site: www.fabianlacey.com   E-mail: mail@fabianlacey.com

ERIC LUTES

Eric was raised in Northern California. During high school, Eric attended the California State Summer School of the Arts and discovered that people could actually have careers in art and design. He attended college in Sacramento where he studied graphic design, and indulged his scientific curiosities with numerous paleontology classes. Eric started work as a graphic design intern at a Sacramento TV station and soon was working full time. After a short stint at Buena Vista Productions on several television shows, he decided to return to school in 2002 to fulfill a lifelong ambition to work in the film industry. Eric moved to Virginia for two years to complete his undergraduate classes, then started at Art Center in 2004, where he studies product and entertainment design.
E-mail: e_lutes@yahoo.com

ERIC NG

Eric Ng was born in Illinois and raised in California. Growing up around comic books and movies, he aspired to be a part of the industry. Childhood memories always revolved around drawing and diving into characters and designs of his imagination. Eric decided that art was his passion and began his schooling at Art Center, studying Industrial Design and Entertainment Design in 2004. He credits his knowledge and experiences to all the teachers that have inspired him along the way.

Web site: www.inkwerkz.com   E-mail: ericng@inkwerkz.com

JUSTIN PICHETRUNGSI

Justin was born in Los Angeles in 1986. At an early age, Justin started recording his experiences and surroundings through drawing, including his doctor visits, family vacations, trains, etc. Inspired by his grandfather, a painter in Thailand, he was determined to pursue the visual arts. Justin took classes in painting, figure drawing and comic book design in his teen years. Later, he attended Saturday High classes at Art Center College of Design, where he was subsequently accepted for the transportation design program. For two summers, he has interned at Design Studio Press with Scott Robertson, where he has worked on various video games. He is currently developing the in-house property, Alien Race. Justin is now a product design major, with emphasis in entertainment design.
Web site: www.rungsi.com   E-mail: justinrungsi@gmail.com

students

RAJ RIHAL

Raj spent the majority of his early life wearing a pair of broken glasses with tape holding them together, preparing for the next science fair and being told to "...give us our hostages back." He unsuccessfully pursued a variety of academic subjects ranging from the classical violin to molecular biology at the University of California, San Diego. After a brief stint studying a protein named NFAT, he decided the academic life was not for him. He packed his bags and headed for Australia where for six months he drove a decrepit plumber's van in search of waves. Upon returning to the States, Raj prepared his portfolio for Product Design at Art Center College of Design and has never looked back. He hopes to work in animation one day.

E-mail: Raj_rihal@yahoo.com

SHAE SHATZ

Shae was born in 1982 in California. At an early age, Shae was fascinated with dismantling things and putting them back together. In primary school he began to collect comic books and became fascinated with the power of storytelling and its potential to influence one's imagination. As a product design major at Art Center College of Design, he has drifted from one realm of design to another through both work and educational experiences. Shae interned at Audi in Simi Valley where he had the opportunity to work on the *Roadjet* show car, which debuted in Detroit in 2006. Shae has been working as a freelance designer on projects that include industrial products, cartoons and video games. After graduation, Shae plans to backpack through Europe!

E-mail: thesynthesis@hotmail.com

CRAIG SHOJI

Craig was born in Torrance, California and has basked in the sun all of his life. As a child, he spent his days taking things apart to better understand them, doodling, and making toys to keep himself entertained. He graduated from U.C.L.A. with a B.S. in Design/Media Arts. In 2004, he entered Art Center College of Design, studying industrial design with an emphasis on concept design for the entertainment industry. Since then, Craig has been both fortunate and grateful to have befriended and worked with some of the most amazing talents in the field. Their influence and tutelage has been priceless and he is eternally thankful. Along with his art, Craig also enjoys teaching others and spends what free time he has mentoring high school students.

Web site: www.craji.com   E-mail: craig@craji.com

KEVIN SWARTZ

Kevin Swartz was born and raised in Santa Monica, California and has been drawing ever since he saw creature-concept drawings for Francis Ford Coppola's *Dracula*, when they were shown during the 1993 Academy Awards. He briefly attended Washington University in St. Louis before transferring to Art Center College of Design, where he is ever drawing and painting.

E-mail: kswartz@gmail.com

THOM TENERY

Thom attended the University of Texas, Arlington, where he graduated with a Bachelor of Science in Architecture. While studying architecture he was exposed to a wide range of designers and artists, most notably the works of Syd Mead, whose extraordinary visions of the future and expert illustrations captivated his interest. Thom declined an opportunity to attend graduate school at Columbia and, instead, set his sights on Art Center. His interest in art history, experimental architecture, concept design and illustration led him to Los Angeles to pursue a career in entertainment design. He is currently working on freelance projects and looking for design opportunities across the entertainment spectrum.

Web site: www.thomlab.com   E-mail: ttenery@gmail.com

LIDAT TRUONG

Lidat Truong was born in North Carolina in 1981 but grew up in Southern California for all but the first few months of his life. Growing up, he loved comic books and video games. After attending the University of California, Irvine for several years, he decided to go for what he really wanted to do, built his portfolio and transferred to the Art Center College of Design. He entered the Product Design curriculum with Entertainment Design as the goal and quickly switched to the new Entertainment Design track when the opportunity presented itself. He is still building his skills through work and Art Center to achieve his goal of becoming a successful concept artist in the entertainment field.

Web site: www.lidatdesign.com   E-mail: lidatdesign@gmail.com

GINO WHITEHALL

Gino Whitehall was born in Healdsburg, California. He spent his childhood reading comic books, drawing his favorite heroes, and creating his own. Upon completion of high school, he moved to the Los Angeles area and enrolled at a local community college with hopes of becoming a product designer. It was here that he was introduced to entertainment design. He began taking as many art class-es as he could to create an admission portfolio for Art Center. In the fall of 2004, he began his first term. Gino is currently pursuing his Illustration degree through the Entertainment Design track. He intends to work in games, film or comics upon graduation.

Web site: www.whitehallstudios.com   E-mail: Gino@Whitehallstudios.com

PATRICK WORSHAM

Patrick was born and raised in Texas. As a child, he loved being able to draw and design. He enjoyed looking at comic book art and loved the work of illustrators. Trained as a graphic designer, Patrick worked for 10 years at an automotive news-paper in Dallas called *Auto Revista*. He was intrigued while looking at amazing sketches of cars, people and products, but never thought of doing it for a living until recently. While working at the newspaper, he took drawing classes at the local community college where a great teacher named Jim Stover inspired him to be an artist/designer. Though it's been a hard road getting to this point in his pursuit of a new career, it's been a very rewarding experience.

E-mail: iamthelighthose@yahoo.com

VICTORIA YING

Victoria Ying was born in Burbank and raised in the small Southern Californian city of Glendora. She attended classes at Art Center's Saturday High program during high school. Afterwards, she began attending Art Center's bachelor's degree program. During her second term at the school, she decided to apply for the new Entertainment Design program. Being mostly interested in comic books, she found that entertainment was a much more exciting route and continues to enjoy the program at Art Center.

Web site: www.victoriaying.net   E-mail: victoria@victoriaying.net

faculty

ALP ALTINER

Alp is an award-winning visual FX artist with over nine years of experience in visual development work for film/TV/commercials and video game-related creations. He is both a 2-D and 3-D artist; specializing in matte painting, concept design, 3-D modeling, texturing and lighting using Adobe Photoshop, Painter, Maya and Z-Brush. Recent films he has worked on include: *X3, Frank Miller's 300, Aeon Flux, Fantastic Four, The Fog, Van Helsing, The Exorcist* and *The Day After Tomorrow*. Alp has also designed for such video game companies as Microsoft, Midway Games, Majesco, Eidos, TimeGate Studios and Monolith.

Web site: www.alpaltiner.com   E-mail: alpvfx@gmail.com

THOMAS BERTLING

Originally from Germany, Thomas was trained as a cabinetmaker. Furniture wasn't enough to keep him completely interested, so off he went to Art Center College of Design for a degree in product design, obtained in 2000. He's done concept and design work for Disney, Belli e Forti, Brown Jordan, Elite Manufacturing, Moen Fixtures, Pixar Film properties, Mattel, and others. He's happiest when diversifying his talents over a wide range of projects, which currently include the development of a series of medical instruments, designing a luxury dog bed, and improving his photography skills.

Web site: www.thomasworks.com   E-mail: t_bertling@gmx.net

REY BUSTOS

Rey Bustos graduated Art Center with a B.F.A. His clients have included LA Gear, Pepsi, USC Medical Center, LA Weekly, The Plain Truth, Pasadena Weekly, West Side Weekly, The Independent Magazine and Location Update Magazine. Rey has exhibited at several galleries in California including the Reid Gallery in Carmel, Random Gallery in Highland Park and Ground Floor 100 Gallery in Pasadena. He is represented by San Marino Gallery in San Marino, California and instructs at Art Center in the Foundation Studies department.

Web site: www.reybustos.com   E-mail: rey@reybustos.com

KEVIN CHEN

Kevin received his B.F.A. in Illustration at Art Center. He has worked on such projects as *Call of Duty* (PS2 video game), *Medal of Honor: Frontline* (PS2 video game), *The Thing* (Xbox video game), *Starship Trooper: Roughneck* (TV show), and the animated film, *Hunchback of Notre Dame*. Previous clients include Infinity Ward, Spark Unlimited, Electronic Arts, Universal Interactive, Digital Domain, Sony Entertainment, and Walt Disney Feature Animation. Kevin has been teaching drawing since 1997 for places such as The Gnomon Workshop, L.A. Academy of Figurative Art, Walt Disney Feature Animation, and DreamWorks Interactive.

Web site: home.earthlink.net/~kevinchen9   E-mail: kevinchen9@earthlink.net

MARK GOERNER

Mark is one of L.A.'s leading concept artists, and has done design content and illustration work for the television, film, automotive, theme park, and gaming industries. In 1996, Mark graduated with distinction from Art Center College of Design in transportation design and an emphasis on entertainment design. Since then he has worked with BMW/Designworks, Coca-Cola, Rhythm & Hues, Disney, Kraft, Honda, and Intel. His current focus is on designing architectural spaces, props, transportation, and characters for such films as *Minority Report, Constantine, X2: X-Men United, Superman Returns,* and *Battle Angel*.

Web site: www.grnr.com   E-mail: mark@grnr.com

BOB KATO

Bob received his B.F.A. at Art Center and his clients have included Adweek, Automobile Magazine, Boston Globe, Creativity, Mother Jones, Tennis, The Grammys, National Lampoon, Playboy Jazz Festival, Spin, Spy, Smithsonian Institution, and the Florida Aquarium. Drawing workshops for Walt Disney Feature Animation, Walt Disney Consumer Products, Disney Online, and Universal Studios Creative. He has authored three instructional DVDs for The Gnomon Workshop and has won awards from the Society of Illustrators and Communication Arts.

Web site: www.thedrawingclub.com   E-mail: info@thedrawingclub.com

RICHARD KEYES

Richard Keyes graduated Art Center with a B.F.A. and went on to establish his own design firm, Keyes Design, after designing for such companies as Steven Jacobs, Fulton & Green and The Graphics Studio. Clients of Richard have included Warner Bros. Records, Guess? Jeans, Convergent Technologies, His Holiness the Dalai Lama, Empire Berol (color consulting), Los Angeles Housing Department and Parsons Engineering (design consultant). After teaching at CSU Los Angeles, Los Angeles Valley Community College and UCLA Extension, Richard now instructs at Art Center in the Foundation Studies department.

E-mail: rkeyes@artcenter.edu

HONG LY

Educated at Art Center, Hong has worked for seven years as a game developer, specializing in character visual development. Clients have included GT Interactive, Lucas Arts, Electronic Arts, THQ and various other publishers and developers. He has taught figure drawing and character design at Associates in Arts.

Web site: www.characterdesigns.com   E-mail: hong@www.characterdesigns.com

EMIL MERTZEL

Emil Mertzel holds a Masters in architecture from the Massachusetts Institute of Technology. He is an architect and designer interested in the relationship of emotion and communication in design. Formerly working for Eric Owen Moss Architects, Emil is now cofounder of his own firm: Lookinglass Architecture & Design. Recent projects include: SIVA - Published in D'A (Taiwan), 2003; SECCA Home Housing Project competition, 2003; GEM competition, 2002; Santa Monica Residence, 2001. Emil teaches in the Environmental Design department at Art Center.

Web site: www.lookinglass.us

GARY MEYER

Gary has been involved in painting, illustration, graphic arts and sculpture since 1960. The first recipient of the Stan Reckless Scholarship and a graduate of Art Center College of Design (B.F.A. with Honors) with additional studies at Chouinard Art Institute, he served as a motion picture production illustrator for Universal Studios. He established his own studio in 1972. Gary's career includes credits on *Star Wars, 2010* and *The Thing*, as well as a 30-year relationship with Universal Studios designing theme park rides.

E-mail: gmeyer@artcenter.edu

NEVILLE PAGE

Neville was educated at Art Center College of Design. Although his major was product design, he has always gravitated towards entertainment. Neville has found himself involved with quite a variety of projects, from creature design and sculpture to conceptual design and engineering. His clients have included Universal Studios, Warner Bros., 20th Century Fox, Mattel, BMW and the films *Minority Report* and *The Chronicles of Narnia: The Lion, the Witch and the Wardrobe*. He is currently involved with the new film project by James Cameron, *Project 880*. Neville has also taught at Otis College, The Gnomon Workshop and corporate workshops.

Web site: www.nevillepage.com

NICK PUGH

Nick Pugh has had a passion for creativity and art his entire life. He currently teaches Originality at Art Center College of Design. For the past ten years, he has been a lead concept artist for the visual effects studio Rhythm & Hues. Recent film projects include *The Chronicles of Narnia*, *Fast and Furious 3*, *Serenity*, and *Superman Returns*. He also creates unique, personal concept cars and vehicular sculptures. His work has appeared in numerous publications and television shows. He holds a B.S. in Transportation Design from Art Center. Nick lives with his wife and daughter in Long Beach, California.

Web site: www.nickpugh.com   E-mail: nick@nickpugh.com

ROBH RUPPEL

Robh Ruppel graduated from Art Center with a B.F.A. and now teaches in the Illustration department. He has also worked as an art director for Walt Disney Features Animation. Projects included *Brother Bear*, *The Emperor's New Groove*, *Tarzan* and *Treasure Planet* among others.

Web site: www.robhruppel.com   E-mail: robhrr@yahoo.com

SCOTT ROBERTSON

Scott is a concept designer, teacher, publisher and graduate of Art Center with a B.S. in Transportation Design. Scott has designed a variety of wheelchairs, bicycles and helmets. In 1995, he began teaching at Art Center in Switzerland and has been instructing tomorrow's designers ever since. Currently, Scott is Program Director of the entertainment design department at Art Center. He is instrumental in developing and implementing the curriculum that will create the concept designers of the future. Dedicated to art and education, Scott founded Design Studio Press, with 17 books currently in print.

Web site: www.drawthrough.com   E-mail: scott@drawthrough.com

CHRISTIAN L. SCHEURER

Christian was born in Bern, Switzerland. As the son of a zoologist father and an artist mother, he lived in many countries, from the bush in South Africa to the Seychelle Islands. After winning the Philip Morris Award for his graphic novels and working on movies and award-winning commercials in Europe, he was struck by lightning. He then decided to pursue a career in Hollywood as a concept artist where he has worked on some of the most innovative movies, games, and commercials in the entertainment industry as a conceptual designer, matte painter, and art director.

Web site: www.christianlorenzscheurer.com   E-mail: cscheurer@earthlink.net

Start Your Engines:
surface vehicle sketches & renderings
from the drawthrough collection

ISBN-10: 1-9334-9213-9
ISBN-13: 978-1-933492-13-1

Lift Off:
air vehicle sketches & renderings
from the drawthrough collection

ISBN-10: 1-9334-9215-5
ISBN-13: 978-1-933492-15-5

Monstruo:
the art of carlos huante
ISBN-10: 0-9726-6762-8

Mas Creaturas:
monstruo addendum
ISBN-10: 1-9334-9207-4

The Art of Darkwatch
ISBN-10: 1-9334-9201-5

Entropia: a collection of
unusually rare stamps
ISBN-10: 1-933492-04-X

LA/SF:
a sketchbook from california
ISBN-10: 1-9334-9210-4

Concept Design 2
ISBN-10: 1-9334-9202-3

Quantum Dreams:
the art of stephan martinière
ISBN-10: 0-9726-6767-9

Quantumscapes:
the art of stephan martinière
ISBN-13: 978-1-933492-51-3

Daphne 01:
the art of daphne yap
ISBN-10: 1-9334-9209-0

Doodles:
200 5-minute doodles
ISBN-13: 978-1-933492-22-3

The Skillful Huntsman
ISBN-10: 0-9726-6764-4

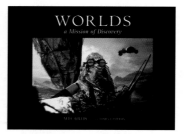

Worlds: a mission of discovery
ISBN-10: 0-9726-6769-5

AVP:
the creature effects of a.d.i.
ISBN-10: 0-9726-6765-2

To order additional copies of this book
and to view other books we offer,
please visit:

www.designstudiopress.com

For volume purchases and resale
inquiries please e-mail:

info@designstudiopress.com

Or you can write to:
Design Studio Press
8577 Higuera Street
Culver City, CA 90232
tel 310.836.3116
fax 310.836.1136

Luminair: techniques of
digital painting from life
ISBN 13: 978-1-933492-24-7